C000259701

WORCESTER
Droitwich Spa, Evesham & Great Malvern

Badsey	17	Malvern Wells	26
Barbourne	6	North Malvern	21
Broadway	29	Northwick	2
Callow End	13	Offenham	18
Cherry Orchard	11	Pershore	28
City Centre	30	Pinvin	28
Colwall Stone	25	Pound Bank	24
Diglis	6	Poolbrook	24
Dines Green	5	Powick	10
Droitwich Spa	15	Rainbow Hill	7
Evesham	17	Rushwick	9
Fernhill Heath	3	Tenbury Wells	29
Great Malvern	21	Trotshill	8
Hallow	1	Upper Colwall	23
Hampton Lovett	15	Upper Howsell	21
Hindlip	4	Upton upon Severn	27
Holly Green	27	Warndon	8
Kempsey	14	West Malvern	23
Lower Broadheath	1	Whittington	12
Malvern Link	22	Wychbold	15

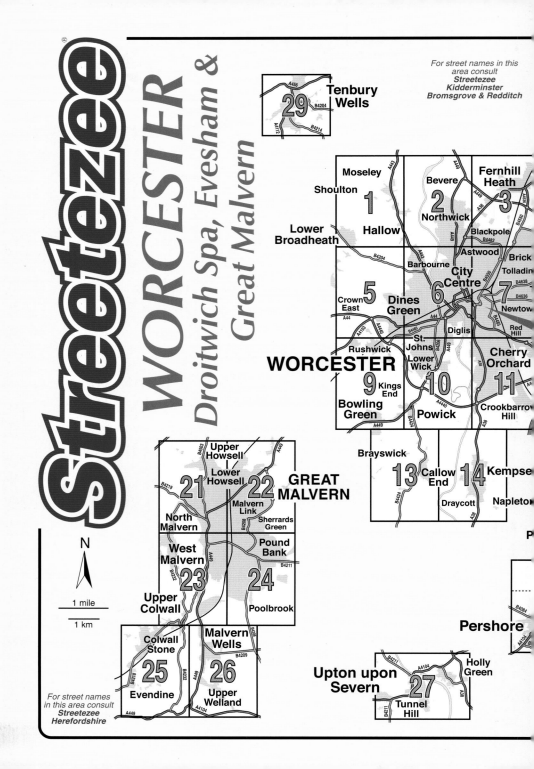

Wychbold **5 15**

Hampton Lovett
DROITWICH SPA **15** Hill End

Newtown
Witton **16**
Primsland

4

Business Parks

6

Wood-green

8

For street names in this area consult
Streetezee
Kidderminster Bromsgrove
& Redditch

Whittington **12**

Worcester City Centre

30

Chadbury
17 **18** Offenham

28

EVESHAM

19 **20** **17**
Hampton Owletts End **Badsey**
Four Pools

For street names in this area consult
Streetezee
Cheltenham &
the Cotswolds

Broadway **29**

Key to street plans

Street plans drawn at a scale of 4 inches to 1 mile

M4	Motorway
A48	A road (Trunk road)
B4281	B road
	Through road
	Dual carriageway
- - - - - -	Track
....	Footpath
	Railway/Station
	Urban area
	Recreation ground
	Woods and forest
✚	Health centre
H A&E	Hospital/A&E dept.
	Petrol station
☉ ✝ ✡	Places of worship
	Police station
⊠	Post Office
((	Telephone/Emergency
T	Toilet facility
P	Car parks (major)
🚐 Δ	Caravan/camp site
i	Information centre
🛆	Picnic site
P&R	Park & Ride
⛳	Golf course
M 🎭	Museum/Theatre
🍺 🏨	Public house/Hotel
▲ YHA	Youth Hostel
42 41 43	House numbers

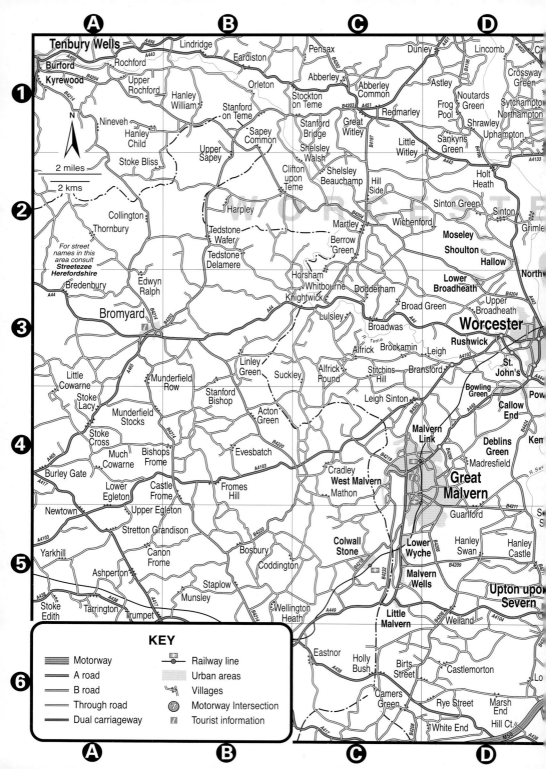

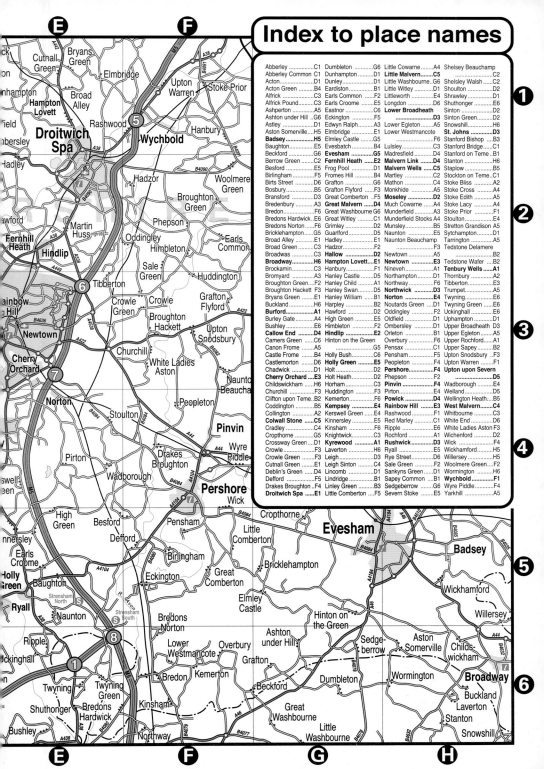

Index to place names

Abberley C1
Abberley Common ...C1
Acton....................D1
Acton Green B4
Alfrick C3
Alfrick Pound.........C3
Ashperton A5
Ashton under Hill ...G6
Astley D1
Aston Somerville....H5
Badsey................H5
Baughton...............E5
Beckford G6
Berrow Green C2
Besford E5
Birlingham F5
Birts Street D6
Bosbury................B5
Bransford D3
Bredenbury A3
Bredon.................D3
Bredons Hardwick ..E6
Bredons Norton F6
Bricklehampton G5
Broad Alley E1
Broad Green C3
Broadwas C3
Broadway.............H6
Brockamin C3
Bromyard A3
Broughton Green....F2
Broughton Hackett F3
Bryans Green E1
Buckland H6
Burford...............A1
Burley Gate A4
Bushley E6
Callow End D4
Camers Green C6
Canon Frome A5
Castle Frome B4
Castlemorton........D6
Chadwick D1
Cherry Orchard E3
Childswickham H5
Churchill F3
Clifton upon Teme..B1
Coddington B5
Collington A2
Colwall Stone C5
Cradley C4
Cropthorne G5
Crossway Green D1
Crowle.................F3
Crowle Green F3
Cutnall Green E1
Deblin's Green D4
Defford F5
Drakes Broughton..F4
Droitwich Spa E1

Dumbleton G6
Dunhampton D1
Dunley.................D1
Eardiston..............B1
Earls Common F2
Earls Croome E5
Eastnor C6
Eckington F5
Edwyn Ralph A3
Elmbridge E1
Elmley Castle G5
Evesbatch B4
Evesham.............G5
Fernhill Heath E2
Frog Pool D1
Fromes Hill B4
Grafton G6
Grafton Flyford F3
Great Comberton ..F5
Great Washbourne G6
Great Witley C1
Grimley D2
Guarlford C3
Hadley.................E1
Hadzor.................F2
Hallow D2
Hampton Lovett..E1
Hanbury...............F1
Hanley Castle D5
Hanley Child A1
Hanley Swan........D5
Hanley William B1
Harpley A5
Hawford D2
High Green E5
Himbleton E2
Hindlip...............E2
Hinton on the Green
..................G5
Holly Bush...........C6
Holly Green E5
Holt D2
Holt Heath D1
Horham C3
Huddington E2
Kemerton F6
Kempsey.............E4
Kerswell Green E4
Kinnersley E5
Kinsham E6
Knightwick............C3
Kyrewood A1
Laverton H6
Leigh C3
Leigh Sinton C3
Lincomb D1
Lindridge B1
Linley Green B3
Little Comberton....F5

Little Cowarne.......A4
Little Malvern.......C5
Little Washbourne..G6
Little Witley D1
Littleworth E4
Longdon...............D5
Lower Broadheath
.....................D3
Lower Egleton A5
Lower Westmancote
Lulsley.................C3
Madresfield D4
Malvern Link.......D4
Malvern Wells C5
Martley C2
Mathon C4
Monkhide A5
Moseley.............D2
Much Cowarne A4
Munderfield A4
Munderfield Stocks A4
Munsley................B5
Naunton B5
Naunton Beauchamp
.....................F3
Newtown A5
Newtown.............E3
Nineveh A1
Northampton A4
Northway..............F6
Northwick...........D3
Norton.................E4
Noutards Green A5
Oddingley.............F2
Oldfield D1
Ombersley D1
Orleton B1
Overbury F6
Pensax B2
Pensham F5
Peopleton F4
Pershore.............F4
Phepson E2
Pinvin................F4
Pirton..................E4
Powick.................D4
Rainbow Hill E3
Rashwood.............E1
Red Marley C1
Ripple...................E6
Rochford A1
Rushwick...........D3
Ryall E6
Rye Street............D6
Sale Green F2
Sankyns Green A5
Sapey Common B1
Sedgeberrow........G6
Severn Stoke E5

Shelsley Beauchamp
.....................C2
Shelsley Walsh C2
Shoulton D2
Shrawley..............D1
Shuthonger..........E6
Sinton D2
Sinton Green.........D2
Snowshill..............H6
St. Johns D3
Stanford Bishop B3
Stanford Bridge.....C1
Stanford on Teme..B1
Stanton H6
Staplow................B5
Stockton on Teme..C1
Stoke Bliss A2
Stoke Cross A4
Stoke Edith A4
Stoke Lacy A4
Stoke Prior F1
Stoulton E4
Stretton Grandison A5
Sytchampton........D1
Tarrington A5
Tedstone Delamere
.....................B2
Tedstone Wafer B2
Tenbury Wells A1
Thornbury A2
Tibberton.............E3
Trumpet A5
Twyning................E6
Twyning Green E6
Uckinghall E6
Uphampton D1
Upper Broadheath D3
Upper Egleton A5
Upper Rochford.....A1
Upper Sapey B2
Upton Snodsbury ..F3
Upton Warren F1
Upton upon Severn
.....................D5
Wadborough E4
Welland D5
Wellington Heath...B5
West Malvern.......C4
Whitbourne C3
White End D6
White Ladies Aston F3
Wichenford D2
Wick F4
Wickhamford........H5
Willersey..............H5
Woolmere Green...F2
Wormington H6
Wychbold F1
Wyre Piddle.........F4
Yarkhill A5

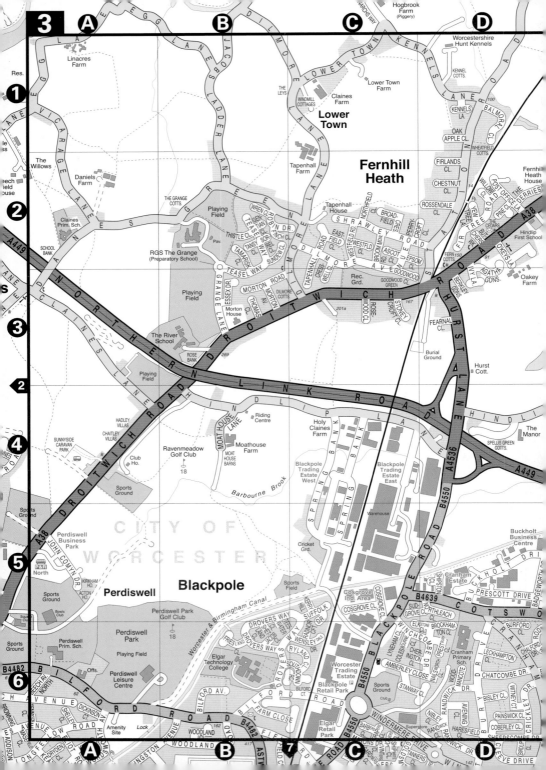

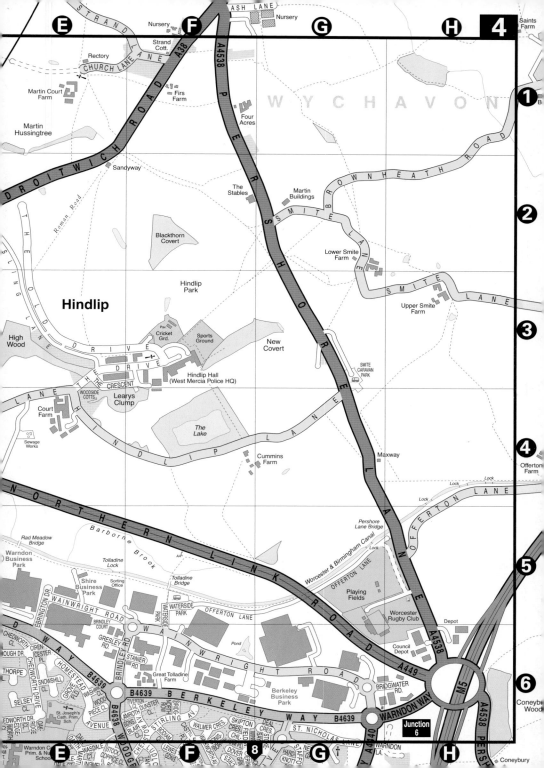

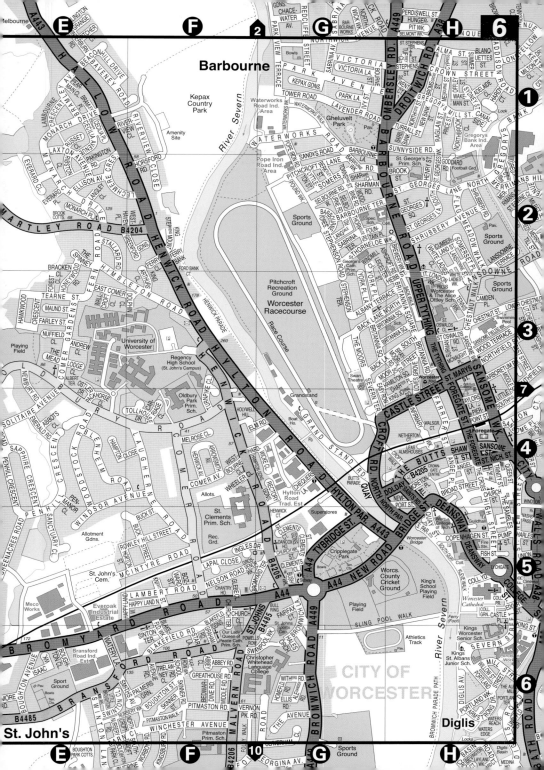

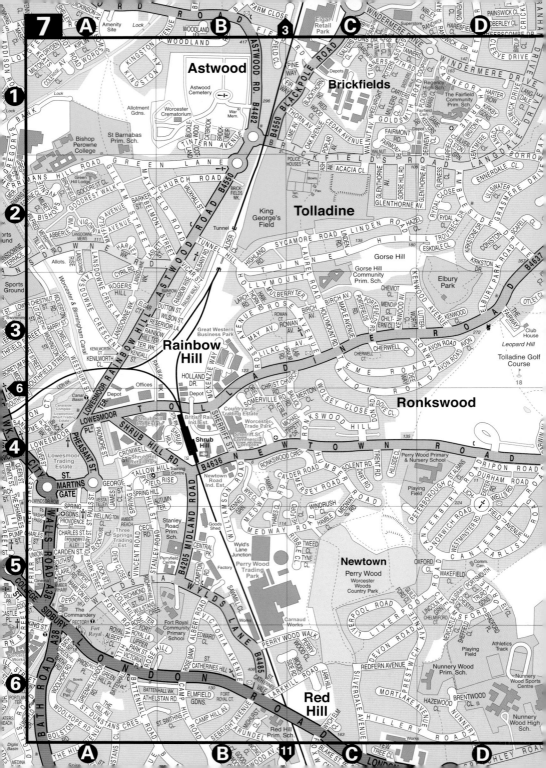

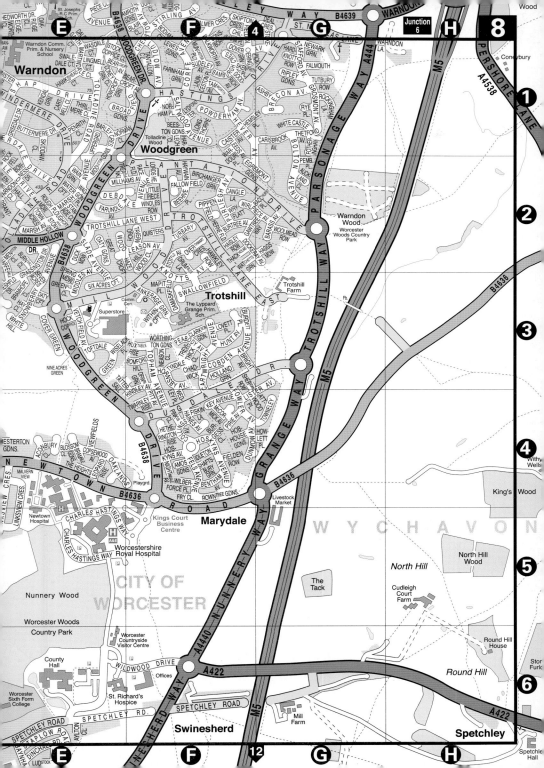

9

A
B
5
C
D

Pond

Grove Farm Reservoir

NEWLAND CRES

NSFOR

Grd.

BRANSFORD ROAD

B4485

A4440

1

Tudor Mount

BRANSFORD ROAD

A4103

BROADMORE GRN

TOLL

HOLLY TREE LA

WHITE HALL CL

BARADINE

MINETT AV

ORCHARD

GRANGE LANE

CORONATION AV.

CHRISTINE AV.

VIVIAN AV.

CHRISTINE AVENUE

Rushwick Prim. Sch.

50

UPPER WICK LANE

Playing Field

Pav.

Upper Wick

Ps.

Broadmore Green

Rushwick

2

River Teme

sford

TAN HOUSE COTTS

Tan House Farm

TAN HOUSE LA.

Upper Wick Farm

Wick Episcopi

Fish Pond

3

Bransford Court

Foxholes Wood

M A L V E R N

H I L L S

dleyard pppice

4

Hill End Cottage

Lord's Wood

Dawes Hill Farm

LANE

Queensbury House

Pond House

Post House

Dawshill

Dawshill House

Bank Farm

HAM LANE ROAD

5

Bush Hill Coppice

Res.

Bush Hill House

Kings End

43

King's End Ho.

97

KINGS END RD.

KINGS END ROAD

MOAT CT.

Colletts Green Farm

Collett's Green

Bowling Green

COLLETTS GREEN RD.

COLLETTS GREEN ROAD

SPARROWHALL LANE

BOWLING GRN RD.

THE GREENWAY

THE PARK

THE ORCHARD

THE LANDS

DRIVE

BRAMLEY CL.

68

OLD MALVERN RD.

OLD MALVERN ROAD

Powick Prim. Sch.

MALVERN ROAD

6

Elms

Mast

MALVERN ROAD

A449

BASTONFORD

BASTONFORD

RUSSELL

CHARLES

PRICE RUPERT AV.

KINGS

HAMILTON CL.

HOSPITAL LA.

13

LODGE FARM COTTAGES

A
B
C
D

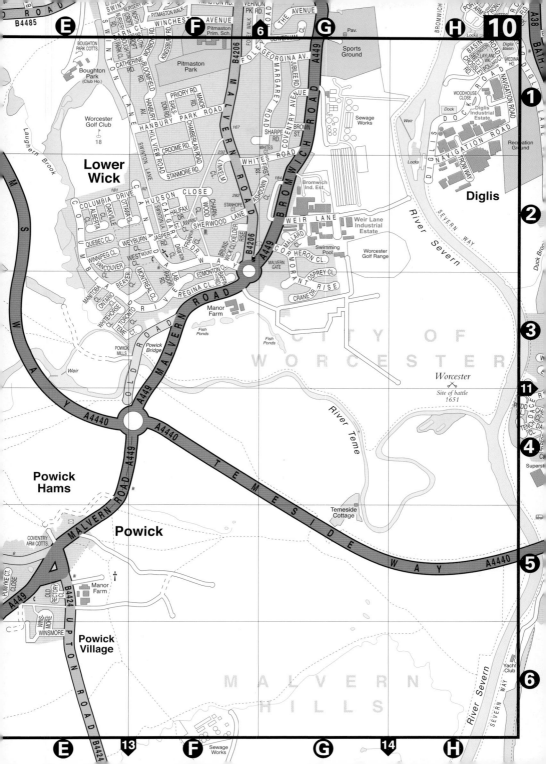

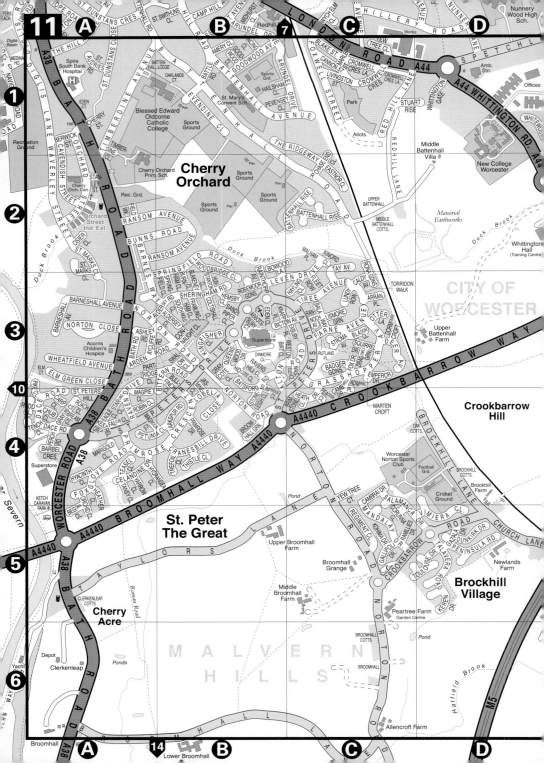

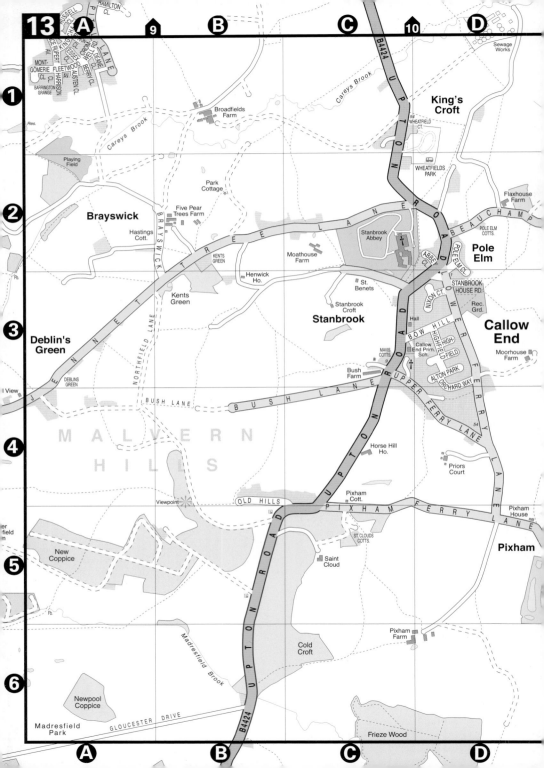

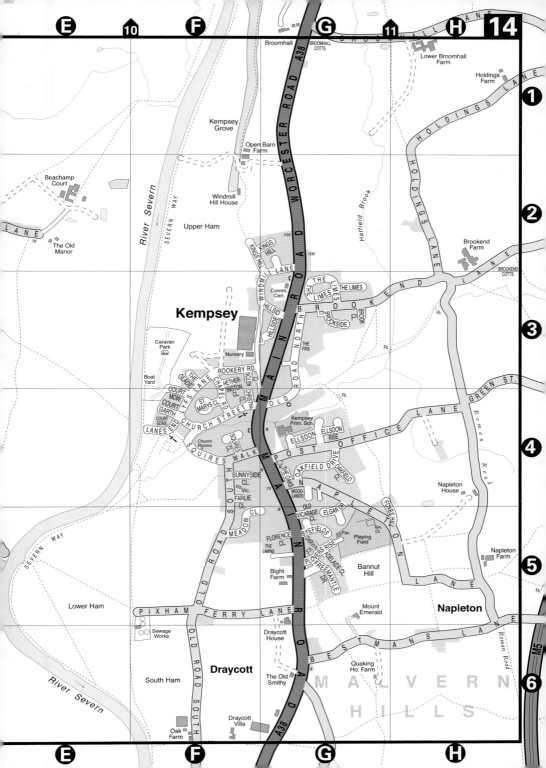

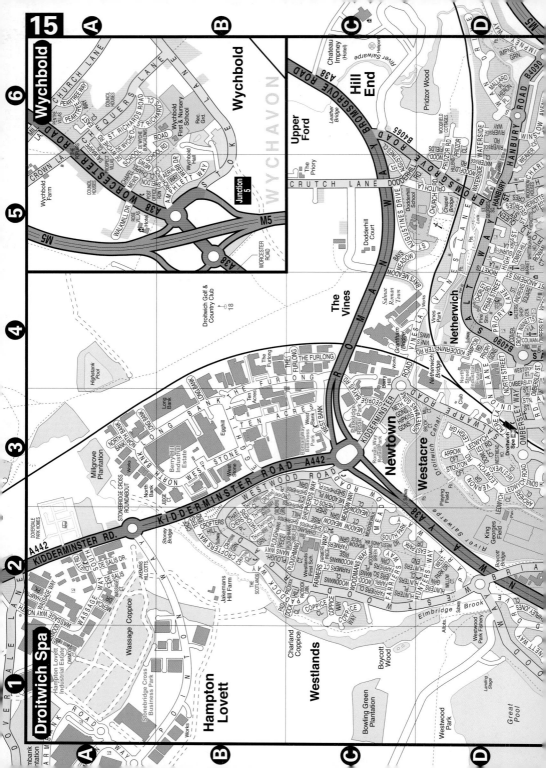

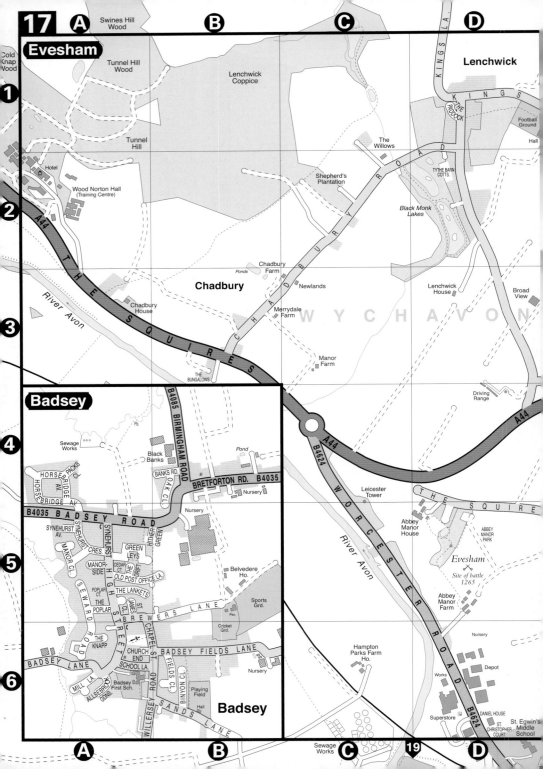

E   F   G   H

CHURCH
WALK

Pond

Lake

Dismantled Railway

River Avon

Harvington Brook

Norton

New Farm

B4088

A46

EVESHAM ROAD

LLOYD CLOSE

BYRD ROW

ST. EGWINS

HEATHFIELD ROAD

Pond

1

Nursery

Nu

2

Hawter

Newlands

Vale View Farm

Court Farm

Offenham

Reservoir

Nursery

Nurse

3

Orchards Farm

Sport Field

Little Twyford Ho.

Vale Wildlife Visitors Centre

Reservoir

GIBBS LANE

COURT LA.

CHURCH ST.

BRIGHTON COTTS.

BRIAR LEA

AVON COURT

COURT COTTS.

MAIN STREET

Nursery

Nursery

THREE COCKS LANE

Res.

B4088

A46

The Hollands

Miniature Railway

Evesham Country Park

Hotel

CHERRY CL.

Offenham First Sch.

MYATT RD.

OLD SCHOOL CL.

Hall

Cricket Grd.

NORVAL CRES.

Rec. Grd.

AVON CROFT

ST. MILBURGH CL.

THE PASSAGE

Nursery

4

A4184

GREENHILL

Twyford

EVESHAM ROAD

MYATT RD.

MYATT ROAD

Nurseries

Nursery

Dead Men's Ait

FERRY LANE

BOAT LANE

MAIN STREET

NEW RD.

LEASOWES ROAD

PIKE COTTS.

BLAYNEYS LANE

ABBOTSWOOD

SIMON DE MONTFORT DR.

Oxstalls Cottage

BOAT LANE

Offenham Ferry

LABURNUM COTTS.

KNOWLEDGE COTTS.

Laurel Nurseries

BARN CROFT MEWS

MILL LANE

LAURELS ROAD

LAURELS AV.

THE CROS

Nurseries

5

119

GREENHILL

Oxstalls Farm

Broadway Brook

Faulk Mill

Pond

B4510

6

PARK ROAD

PRINCE HENRY'S CL.

PRINCE EDWARDS CL.

GREENHILL TER.

COLLINSFIELD

Greenhill

Green Hill Sch.

LANESFIELD PK.

33

CROFT ROAD

THE GARD

BALMORAL CL.

River Avon

Parks Farm

Totterdown

THE PARKS

EVESHAM ROAD

B4510

Depot

Nursery

Nursery

Nursery

Sidi Cotts

E   F   20   G   H

A46

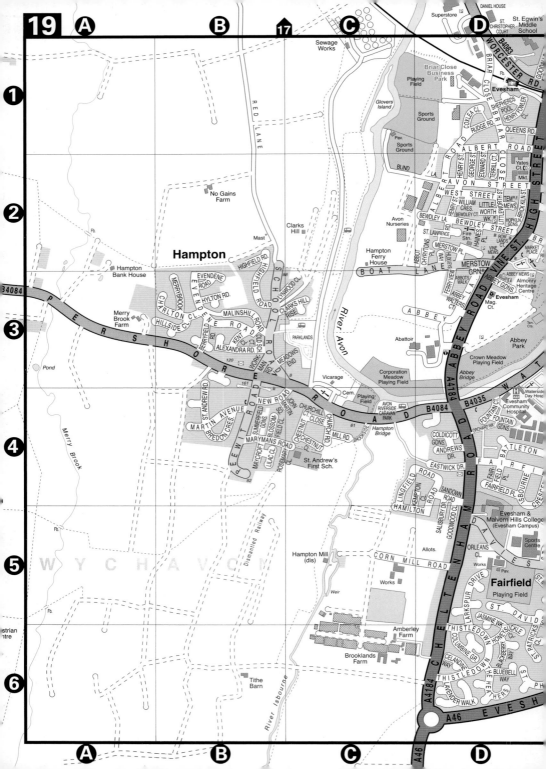

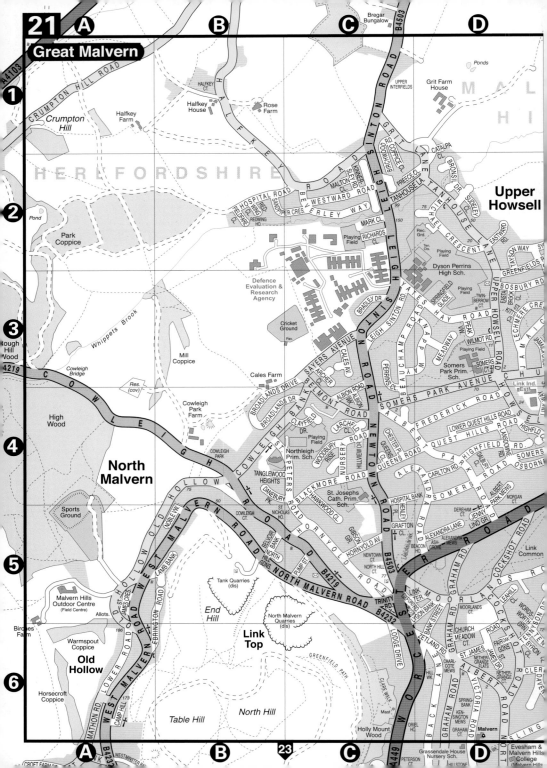

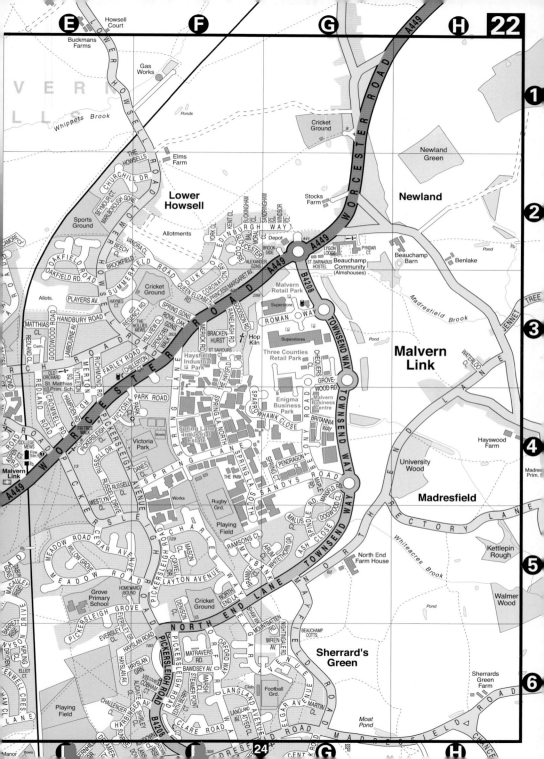

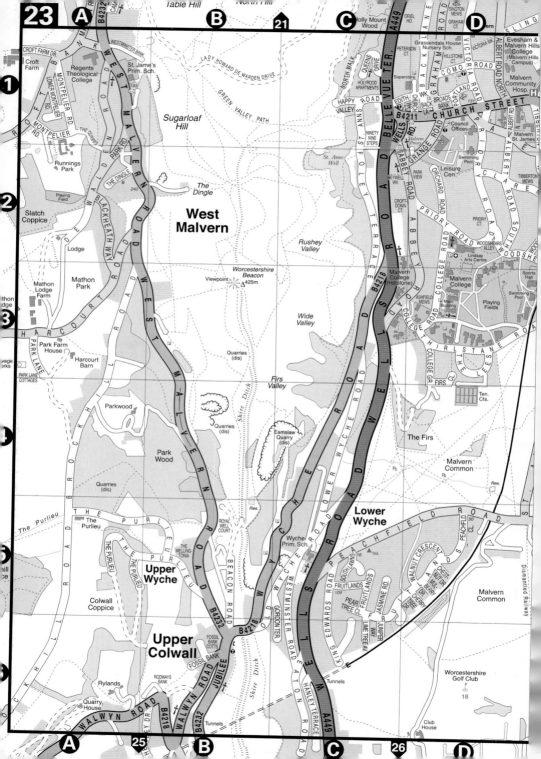

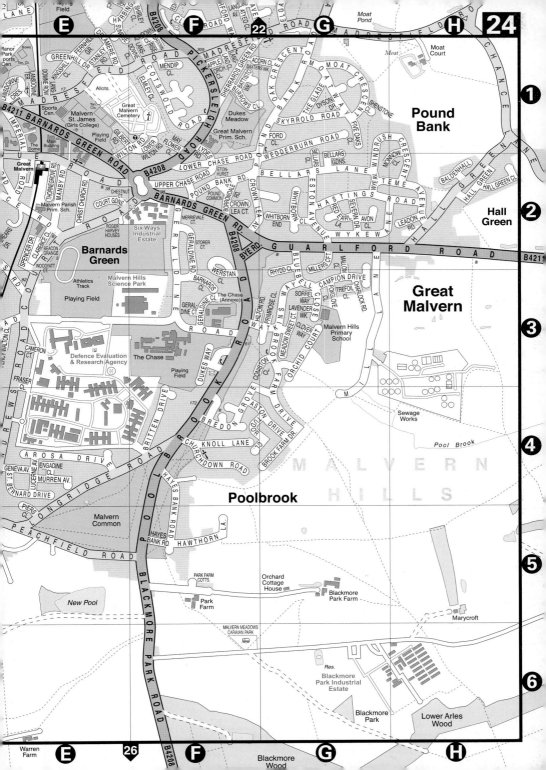

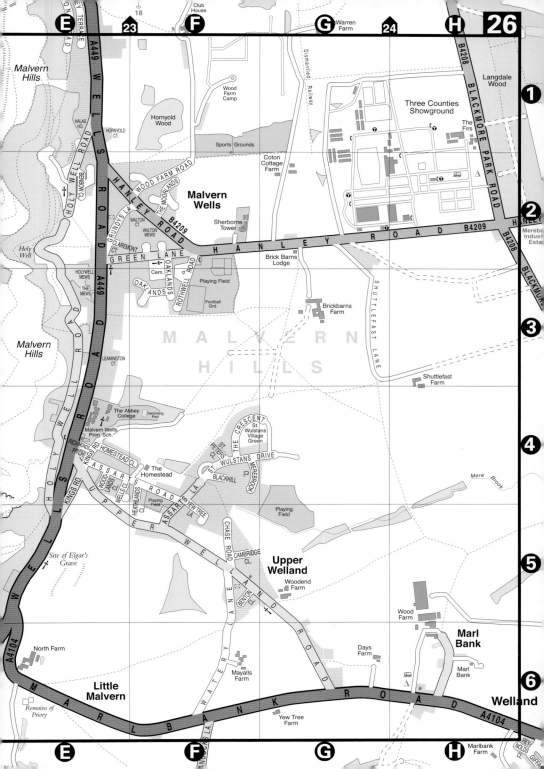

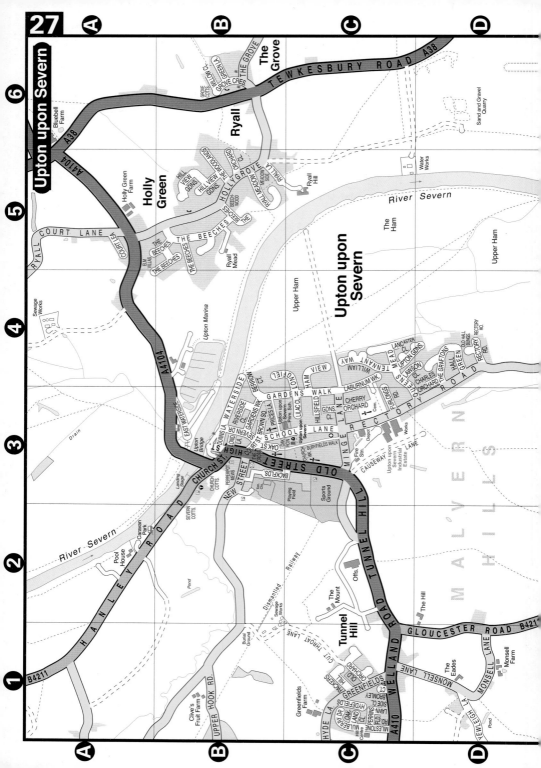

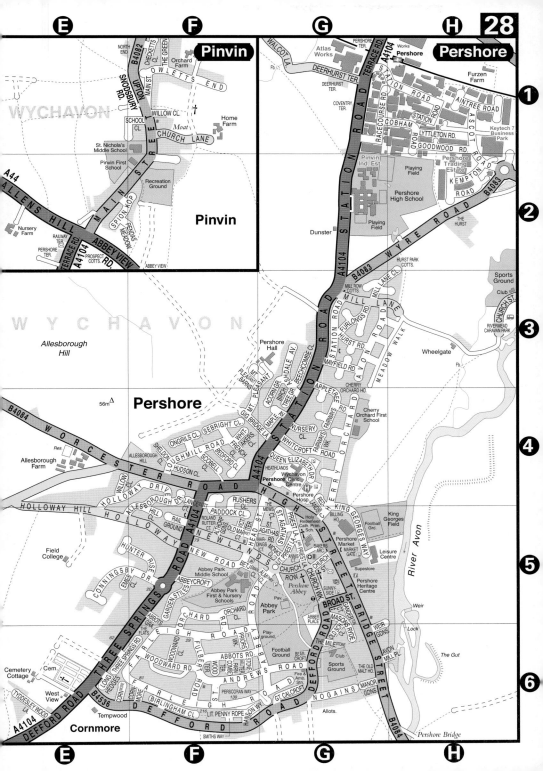

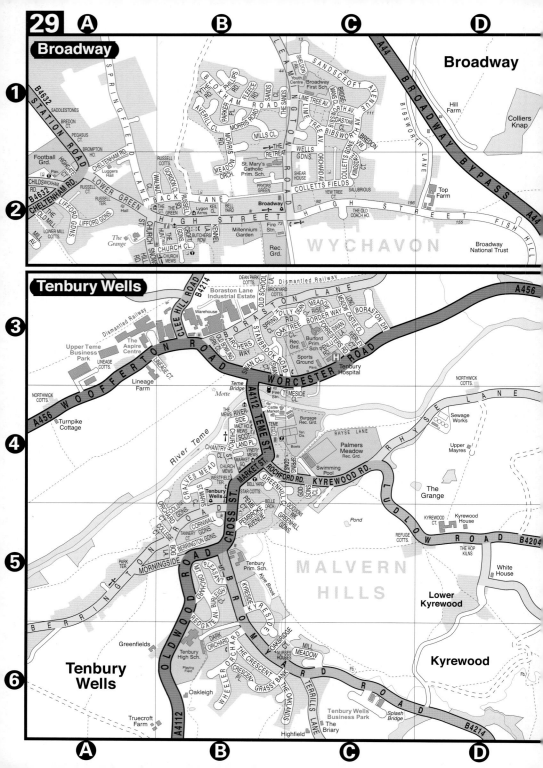

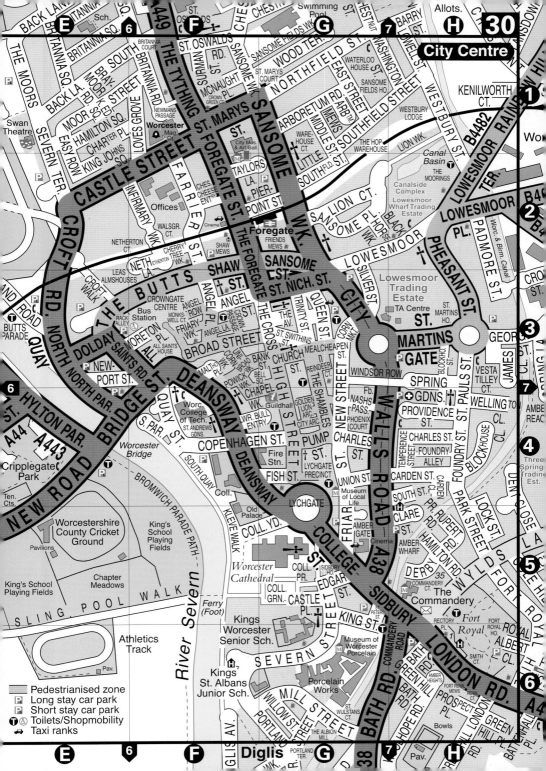

INDEX Abbreviations used

Allot(s).	Allotment(s)	Coll.	College	Fld(s).	Field(s)	Inf.	Infant	Off(s).	Office(s)	S.	South
Amb.	Ambulance	Comm.	Community	Flts.	Flats	Junc.	Junction	Orch(s).	Orchard(s)	Sq.	Square
App.	Approach	Comp.	Comprehensive	Fb(s).	Footbridge(s)	Jun.	Junior	Par.	Parade	Stn.	Station
Arc.	Arcade	Cov.	Covered	Gdns.	Gardens	Lib.	Library	Pk.	Park	St.	Street
Av.	Avenue	Crn.	Corner	Gt.	Great	Lit.	Little	Pass.	Passage	Ten.	Tennis
Br.	Bridge	Cott(s).	Cottage(s)	Gra.	Grange	Lwr.	Lower	Pav.	Pavilion	Ter.	Terrace
Brd.	Broad	Cres.	Crescent	Grn.	Green	Mkt.	Market	Pl.	Place	Up.	Upper
Bldg(s).	Building(s)	Cft.	Croft	Grd.	Ground	Mag.	Magistrates	Pr.	Precinct	Vic.	Vicarage
Bung(s).	Bungalow(s)	Ct.	Court	Gr.	Grove	Mdw(s).	Meadow(s)	Prim.	Primary	Vw.	View
Bus.	Business	Dis.	Disused	Hd.	Head	Mem.	Memorial	Rec.	Recreation	Vlls.	Villas
Cara.	Caravan	Dr.	Drive	Hts.	Heights	Mon.	Monument	Res.	Reservoir	Wk.	Walk
Cem.	Cemetery	E.	East	Hosp.	Hospital	Mt.	Mount	Resid.	Residential	Wy.	Way
Cen.	Centre	Ent.	Enterprise	Ho.	House	N.	North	Rd.	Road	W.	West
Cl.	Close	Est.	Estate	Ind.	Industrial			Sch.	School	Yd.	Yard

Use of this Index:

1. An alphabetical order is followed.
2. Each street name is followed by a map reference giving a page number and coordinates: Abberley Drive **16** G3.
3. Where a street name appears more than once the reference is given: Arundel Drive **7** B6/**11** C1.
4. Names not appearing on the map are shown with an * and the reference of the nearest adjoining street: Abbey House*, St. Wulstans Cl. **20** E6.
5. House numbers along streets are shown: *250*.

A

Abberley Drive **16** G3
Abberley House*, Henwick Rd.
.................................**6** F3
Abberley View **7** A2
Abbey Close (Callow End)
.................................**13** D2
Abbey Close (Worcester) **6** F6
Abbey Gardens **19** D3
Abbey House*,
St. Wulstans Cl. **20** E6
Abbey Lane **19** D3
Abbey Manor Park **17** D5
Abbey Mews **19** D3
Abbey Place **28** G5
Abbey Road (Evesham) **19** D4
Abbey Road (Gt. Malvern)
.................................**23** D2
Abbey Road (Pershore) **28** G6
Abbey Road (Worcester) ..**6** F6
Abbey View **28** F2
Abbey View Road **28** E2
Abbeycroft **28** F5
Abbot Chyrytons Place ..**19** D2
Abbot Park Mews **21** D4
Abbot Walters Court **19** D3
Abbots Close **6** E4
Abbots Grange **28** F5
Abbots Road **28** F6
Abbots Walk **19** D3
Abbotsbury Court **11** B3
Abbotswood **18** E5
Acacia Close **7** C2
Aconbury Close **8** E4
Acorn Close (Colwall) **25** B2
Acorn Close (Gt. Malvern)
.................................**24** F1

Acorn Grove **28** G4
Acre Lane **15** D3
Acton House **3** A5
Addison Road **6** H1
Addyes Green **16** H4
Addyes Way **16** H3
Adelaide Close (Kempsey)
.................................**14** G5
Adelaide Close (Worcester)
.................................**6** H1
Adenbrooke Road **16** E4
Admiral Place **11** C4
Adrian Close **16** F5
Aerial Way **15** B5
Agatha Gardens **3** D3
Aintree Road **28** H1
Albany Road **7** B2
Albany Terrace **6** G3
Albermarle*, Vimiera Close
.................................**11** D5
Albert Park Mews **21** D4
Albert Park Road **21** C4
Albert Road (Colwall) **25** B2
Albert Road (Evesham)
.............................**19** D1/D2
Albert Road (Worcester) ..**7** B6
Albert Road North **21** D6
Albert Road South **23** D1
Albert Street **15** D3
Albert Terrace **6** E3
Albert Villas*, Oldbury Road
.................................**5** D4
Alberta Close **10** E2
Albion Mill, The **30** G6
Albion Road **21** C4
Albion Walk **21** C4
Alder Close **7** B2
Alder Grove (Droitwich) ..**16** G4

Alder Grove (Evesham) ..**20** F5
Alderbrook Road **16** F1
Aldersey Close **11** B3
Aldersey Road **11** B3
Alexander Avenue **16** F2
Alexander Gardens **22** F2
Alexander Road **6** G6
Alexandra Lane **21** D5
Alexandra Mews **21** D5
Alexandra Road (Evesham)
.................................**19** B3
Alexandra Road (Gt. Malvern)
.................................**21** D5
Alicante Close **22** F6
All Saints House **30** F3
All Saints Road **30** E3
Allardene **20** F3
Allee de Dreux*, Bridge St.
.................................**19** D2
Allens Hill **28** E2
Allesborough Drive **28** F5
Allesborough Hill **28** F4
Allsebrook Gardens **17** A6
Alma Street **6** H1
Almond Close **20** F4
Almonry Close **28** F5
Althorp Gardens **28** F5
Alton Park **13** D3
Alton Road **11** B3
Amber Gate **30** G5
Amber Heights **30** H6
Amber Reach **7** A5
Amber Wharf **30** H5
Amberley Close **3** C6
Ambleside Drive **7** D2
Ambrose Close **5** D4
Ambrose Court **5** D4
Amery Close **11** B1

Amos Gardens **8** F4
Amphlett Way **15** B5
Amroth Gardens **4** F6
Anchor House*,
Lowesmoor Ter. **30** H2
Andrew Close **6** E3
Andrews Drive **19** D4
Angel Lane **30** F3
Angel Mall*, Angel Pl. **30** F3
Angel Place **30** F3
Angel Row **30** F3
Angel Street **30** F3
Ankerage Green **8** F3
Ankerdine House*,
Henwick Road **6** F3
Anne Crescent **20** E4
Annis Court **28** G5
Anvil House*, Mill St. **20** E2
Apple Orchard Close **24** F1
Apple Tree Road **28** G3
Arboretum Mews **30** G1
Arboretum Road **30** G1
Archbell Cottages **1** D4
Archer Close (Gt. Malvern)
.................................**21** C3
Archers Close (Droitwich)
.................................**15** D3
Archers Way **29** B3
Arden Road **11** A3
Arkle Close **16** G6
Arkle Road **16** G6
Arlington Court*, Droitwich Rd.
.................................**6** H1
Arlington Grange **2** E6
Armstrong Drive **6** H6
Arosa Drive **24** E4
Arran Place **11** C3
Arrow Croft **15** D3

Arrowsmith Avenue **6** F4
Arum Close **22** G5
Arundel Drive **7** B6/**11** C1
Ascot Close **3** C2
Ascot Road **28** H1
Ash Avenue......................**7** C2
Ash Close **22** G5
Ash Grove (Evesham) **20** F5
Ash Lane **4** F1
Ashby **8** G1
Ashcroft Road **6** G2
Ashdale Avenue **28** G3
Ashdown Close (Gt. Malvern)
...................................**24** F1
Ashdown Close (Worcester)
...................................**10** G2
Ashdown Rise **24** F1
Ashendon Close **16** G4
Ashfield Mews **23** D3
Ashgrove (Gt. Malvern) ..**21** D5
Ashley Road **11** A3
Ashwin House*, Howsell Road
...................................**21** D4
Asparagus Way **20** F6
Aspen Close **20** F5
Aspen Court **22** E4
Assarts Lane **26** F5
Assarts Road...................**26** E4
Aston Close **14** F3
Aston Drive **24** G4
Astwood Court*, Tintern Av.
....**7** B1
Astwood Lane*, Stoke Lane
.....................................**15** B6
Astwood Road **7** B1/B3
Athelstan House*, The Hill Av.
....**7** A6
Athelstan Road **7** A6
Attwood Place **8** F4
Atyeo Close **22** F6
Auckland Close **8** G2
Austen Close **13** A1
Autumn Terrace...............**7** B4
Avening Close **3** D6
Avenue Road (Gt. Malvern)
...................................**23** D1
Avenue Road (Worcester)
....**6** F6
Avenue, The (City Centre)
...................................**30** G3
Avenue, The (St. John's)..**6** G6
Avenue, The (Welland) ..**26** H6
Averill Close **29** B1
Avon Close (Gt. Malvern)
...................................**24** G2
Avon Close (Worcester) ..**7** D3
Avon Court **18** G3
Avon Mill Place **28** G6
Avon Riverside Caravan Park
...................................**19** C4

Avon Road (Pershore) ..**28** G3
Avon Road (Worcester)....**7** C3
Avon Street **19** D2
Avoncroft **18** H4
Avoncroft Court*, Galton Way
...................................**16** E6
Avondale **16** F2
Aycliffe Road **11** A3
Aylton Close **8** E6

B

Bacchurst Place **8** G2
Back Lane (Broadway) ..**29** A2
Back Lane (Gt. Malvern) **21** D6
Back Lane North **6** G3
Back Lane South **30** E1
Back Walk **6** H3
Backfields Lane...............**27** C3
Badger Gardens **11** C3
Badgeworth Drive **3** D5
Badsey Fields Lane.........**17** B6
Badsey Lane. **17** A6/**20** F3
Badsey Road **17** A5/**20** H2
Baffin Road **10** F3
Bagehott Close **16** H3
Bagehott Road **16** H3
Bagshaw Court*,
   Worcester Road **28** F4
Bainbrigge Avenue **16** E5
Baker Street **7** A2
Bakers Arcade **28** G5
Bala Way........................**11** C3
Baldenhall **24** H2
Ballard Close **25** B1
Ballards Drive **25** D1
Balliol Road **7** C4
Balmoral Close (Evesham)
...................................**18** E6
Balmoral Close
   (Fernhill Heath) **3** D1
Balmoral Close (Gt. Malvern)
...................................**22** F2
Bamburgh Crescent..........**8** F1
Bank Street (City Centre)
...................................**30** F3
Bank Street (Gt. Malvern)
...................................**21** D6
Banks Road...................**17** B4
Bankside Close **2** G6
Banner Court*, Castle Street
...................................**20** E2
Baradene Lane **9** C1
Barass Avenue **8** G2
Barbel Crescent.............**11** A4
Barbers Close **3** C6
Barbourne Bank **6** H1
Barbourne Court*,
   Barbourne Crescent..**6** G2
Barbourne Crescent **6** G2
Barbourne Lane **6** G1

Barbourne Road **6** G1
Barbourne Terrace **6** G2
Barbourne Walk **6** G2
Barbourne Works **2** G6
Barley Crescent................**8** E1
Barley Orchard Court.....**20** F3
Barn Close.......................**6** E6
Barn Croft Mews **18** H4
Barnards Close (Evesham)
...................................**20** E4
Barnards Close (Gt. Malvern)
...................................**24** F3
Barnards Green Road **24** E1
Barnes Way....................**11** A2
Barneshall Avenue **11** A3
Barns Croft Way **16** F1
Barrett Rise **22** E6
Barrington Grange..........**13** A1
Barry Street **7** A3
Basin Road **10** H1
Bastonford **9** B6
Bastonford Villas **9** B6
Bath Road
   ....**11** A4/A5/**30** G6/H6
Batsford Road **11** B3
Battenhall Avenue **11** B1
Battenhall Lodge **11** A1
Battenhall Place **7** A6
Battenhall Rise **11** C2
Battenhall Road **7** A6/**11** B1
Battenhall Walk **7** A6
Battisto Walk **24** F1
Battle Road **11** B1
Battleton Road **19** D4/**20** E4
Baveney Road...................**6** E1
Bawdsey Avenue **22** F6
Baxters Walk **24** F1
Bayly Close **20** E4
Baynham Drive **12** E1
Bays Meadow **15** C3
Beach Close **20** E3
Beacon Grange **24** E2
Beacon House.................**21** C5
Beacon Road..................**23** B5
Beaconhill Drive **6** E1
Bearcroft **28** G6
Bearcroft Avenue..............**8** E1
Beauchamp Cottages **22** G6
Beauchamp Lane **13** D2
Beauchamp Road **21** C4
Beaver Close **10** E3
Beckett Close **2** G5
Beckett Drive **2** G5
Beckett Road **2** G5
Bedford Close **28** F4
Bedwardine Road **6** F6
Beech Avenue...................**2** H6
Beech Avenue North **3** A6
Beech Close **22** F1
Beechcombe Close........**28** G3

Beeches, The (Upton) **27** B5
Beeches, The*, Back Lane
...................................**29** A2
Beechwood **27** B5
Beehive Place **8** F2
Beeston Gardens.............**8** F1
Begonia Close **11** A4
Belfry Road **16** G4
Bell Close **1** D4
Bell Lane **5** A1
Bell Square **30** F3
Bell Yard (Broadway) **29** B2
Bell Yard (Tenbury Wells)
...................................**29** B4
Bellars Close **24** G2
Bellars Gardens **24** G2
Bellars Lane **24** G2
Belle Orchard **29** B4
Belle Vue Terrace **23** C1
Belmont Lodge*, Belmont St.
....**7** A2
Belmont Road **21** C4
Belmont Street.................**7** A2
Belmont Walk **2** H6
Belvoir Bank **21** B5
Benbow Close **26** E2
Bentham Avenue **8** F4
Benton Close **26** F5
Berkeleys Court*, Shaw St.
...................................**30** F3
Berkley Gardens **3** D3
Berkley Street **6** G2
Berkley Way **4** F6
Berrill Close **16** F6
Berrington Gardens.........**29** B5
Berrington Mews*,
   Berrington Gdns. **29** B5
Berrington Road **29** A6
Berrow Court **27** B3
Berrow House*, Henwick Rd.
....**6** F3
Berry Close **13** A1
Berryfield Road **19** B3
Berwick Street **11** A1
Bestmans Lane **14** G6
Betjeman Close **28** F5
Betony Road **22** G4
Bevere Close **2** G4
Bevere Close South **2** G4
Bevere Court **2** F3
Bevere Drive **2** G4
Bevere House **2** G2
Bevere Lane **2** G2
Beverley Way **21** C2
Bevington Court **10** H1
Bewdley Court **19** D2
Bewdley Lane **19** D2
Bewdley Street **19** D2
Bibsworth Avenue **29** C1
Bibsworth Lane **29** C1

Bicton Avenue 11 C3
Bilford Avenue 3 B6
Bilford Court 3 C6
Bilford Road........2 H6/3 A6/B6
Billing House 28 G4
Binyon Close 17 B6
Birch Avenue (Evesham)20 G4
Birch Avenue (Worcester) 7 C3
Birch Coppice 16 G4
Birch Tree Grove............28 G4
Birchanger Green 8 F2
Birchfield Close 7 A2
Birchwood Road 21 C1
Birdlip Close 7 D1
Birlingham Close 28 F6
Birmingham Road 17 B4
Bishops Avenue 7 A2
Bisley Close 3 D6
Bittern Road 11 B3
Black & White Cottages..12 E5
Black Horse Walk 30 G2
Blackberry Way 19 D6
Blackfriars Avenue..........16 F3
Blackfriars Court 16 E4
Blackheath Way 23 A2
Blackhill 26 F4
Blackmore Park Road 24 F5
Blackmore Road 21 C4
Blackpole Road........3 C6/7 B1
Blackthorn Close (Evesham)
.....................................20 G4
Blackthorn Road 7 C1
Blackthorne Close (Droitwich)
.....................................16 G5
Blagdon Close 11 C3
Blair Close 4 F6
Blake Avenue 16 F2
Blake Street...................11 C1
Blakefield Gardens 6 F5
Blakefield Road 6 F6
Blakefield Walk 6 F6
Blakeney Close 11 B3
Blandford Close..............26 H6
Blanquettes Avenue 2 H6
Blanquettes Street...........6 H1
Blayneys Lane................18 E5
Blenheim Road 6 E4
Blind Lane 19 D2
Blockhouse Close 30 H4
Blockhouse Street...........30 H3
Bloomfield Road 10 F1
Blossom Close 8 E4
Blossomfield Close 19 B4
Bloxham Road 29 B1
Bluebell Close (Gt. Malvern)
.....................................24 G2
Bluebell Close*, Grove Cres.
.....................................27 B6
Bluebell Way 19 D6
Boat Lane (Evesham) 19 D2

Boat Lane (Offenham) ..18 G4
Bodiam Close 4 F6
Bog Lane 29 B5
Bolston Road....................7 A6
Bolton Avenue..................8 G1
Bomford Hill 8 F3
Bond Street 22 E3
Boraston Drive 29 C3
Boraston Lane 29 B3
Border Way 29 C3
Borrowdale Drive.............7 D2
Borrowdale Road............24 F2
Bosbury Road 21 D3
Boston Lane 19 A2
Boswell Court*, Howsell Road
.....................................21 D2
Boughton Avenue 6 E6
Boughton Close...............6 E6
Boughton Park Close 10 E1
Boughton Park Cottages ..6 E1
Boughton Street...............6 F6
Bourne Close..................16 E4
Bourne Street 6 G1
Bow Hill 13 C3
Bowden Green 16 H4
Bower Hill (Droitwich) 16 F2
Bowers Hill*, Willersey Road
.....................................17 A6
Bowling Green Road 9 B6
Bowness Drive 8 E2
Bowood Lane 11 B3
Bozward Street 6 F5
Bracken Close 6 E2
Brackenhurst 22 F3
Bradford Place 7 D5
Bradley Drive 21 C3
Bramble Close 22 F5
Bramble Gardens 8 E4
Bramhope Close 8 E3
Bramley Avenue 6 E1
Bramley Close 9 C6
Bramley Place 6 E1
Bransford Road
..................5 D6/6 E6/9 A1
Brantwood 8 E2
Brantwood Close............16 G5
Brantwood Road 16 F5
Braymoor Road 30 E1
Brayswick 13 B2
Bream Close 11 A4
Brecon Avenue 8 G1
Brecon Close 16 F1
Bredon Court 29 A1
Bredon Crescent 19 B4
Bredon Grove 24 G4
Bredon View (Broadway)29 C1
Bredon View (Hinton) 19 A4
Brentwood Close..............7 D6
Bretforton Road 17 B4
Brewers Lane 17 A5

Brewery Court*, Bewdley St.
.....................................19 D2
Brewery Walk 6 H2
Briar Close 19 D1
Briar Lea 18 G4
Briar Mill 15 D1
Brick Kiln Street..............19 D2
Brickfields Road 7 B1
Brickfields Walk 7 B2
Brickyard Cottages 29 B3
Bridge Court 20 E3
Bridge Street (Evesham)19 D2
Bridge Street (Pershore) 28 G5
Bridge Street (Worcester) 6 H5
Bridgemans Close..........29 C1
Bridgnorth Row 4 F6
Bridgwater Road 4 G6
Bright Avenue 8 F3
Brighton Cottages 18 G3
Brimstone Close 11 C4
Brindley Court 4 E5
Brindley Road 4 E6
Britannia Court...............30 F1
Britannia Road...............30 F1
Britannia Square....6 G3/30 E1
Britannia Way 22 G4
British Camp Road 25 A6
Britten Drive....................24 F4
Broad Street (City Centre)
.....................................30 F1
Broad Street (Pershore) 28 G5
Broad Walk 30 F3
Broadfield Crescent.........3 C2
Broadfield Gardens 8 F1
Broadheath Close 16 G3
Broadheath Common 5 A2
Broadheath Lane.............1 C5
Broadlands Drive 21 C4
Broadmeadow 16 F3
Broadmore Green 9 B1
Broads Bank 23 D1
Broadway Bypass 29 C1
Broadway Court*,
Snowshill Road....29 A2
Broadway Grove 5 D6
Broadway Road 20 F3/G4
Broadwood Drive............25 C1
Broadwood Park 25 C1
Brockhampton Close........3 D6
Brockhill Cottages 11 D4
Brockhill Lane 11 D4
Brockhill Road 25 C1
Brockweir..........................7 B1
Bromley Court 27 C1
Brompton House 29 A1
Bromsgrove Road 15 D5
Bromsgrove Street 6 H1
Bromwich Lane 6 G6
Bromwich Parade Path ..30 F4
Bromwich Road ...6 G6/10 G2

Bromyard Road
(Tenbury Wells) 29 B5
Bromyard Road (Worcester)
..........................5 C5/6 G5
Bromyard Terrace 6 G5
Bronsil Close 12 E1
Bronsil Drive 21 D2
Brook Close 14 G3
Brook Cottages (Rushwick)
....5 D6
Brook Cottages (Worcester)
....6 G3
Brook Court 15 D3
Brook Farm Drive 24 G3
Brook Street 6 H2
Brookend Cottages 14 H2
Brookend Lane 14 H3
Brookfield 22 E2
Brookmill Close 25 A1
Brookside (Colwall) 25 B2
Brookside (Evesham) 19 C4
Brookside (Gt. Malvern) 22 G2
Brookside (Welland) 26 H6
Brookside Road (Kempsey)
.....................................14 G3
Brookside Road (Worcester)
....5 D4
Brookthorpe Close 3 D6
Broom Meadow Road 3 C2
Broomhall 11 C6
Broomhall Cottages........11 C6
Broomhall Green 11 B4
Broomhall Lane 11 A6
Broomhall Way 11 A5
Broomhill Cottages 14 G1
Brown Square 27 B3
Brown Street 10 G1
Brownes Way 1 D3
Brownheath Road 4 G2
Browning Close 2 H6
Browning Court*, Kipling Cl.
.....................................22 E6
Brunswick Close 10 F2
Buck Street 6 F5
Buckholt Drive 3 D5
Buckingham Close..........22 F2
Buckle Wood 7 B1
Bull Ring 6 G5
Bullfinch Close................11 B3
Bullfinch Close 17 B3
Bungalows, The..............17 B3
Burdett Place 8 F3
Burford Close 3 D6
Burford Gardens 20 E2
Burford Road 20 E3
Burgess Close 8 F4
Burleigh Close 29 B5
Burleigh Road 5 D4
Burlingham Avenue........20 G2
Burlingham Court*, Briar Cl.
.....................................19 D2

Burma Close **20** E4
Burnham Close **11** B3
Burns Road **11** A2
Burnsall Close **8** E2
Burrish Street **16** E4
Burrows Close **24** F1
Burtree Avenue **8** F2
Bury End*, Snowshill Road
....................................**29** A2
Buryfields Walk **27** C3
Bush Lane **13** A4/B4
Bush Walk......................**6** G5
Butchers Row **29** B2
Butchers Walk **3** D2
Butterfly Crescent **20** F3
Buttermere Drive **8** E1
Butterworth House*, Mill St.
....................................**20** E2
Butts Parade.........**6** G4/**30** E3
Butts, The (City Centre)..**30** E3
Butts, The (Droitwich) **16** F2
Bye Road......................**24** F2
Byefields **14** G5
Byfield Rise **7** A4
Byrd Row......................**18** E1
Byron Close (Collett's Green)
....................................**13** A1
Byron Close (Gt. Malvern)
....................................**21** D6

C

Cage, The*, Market Sq...**29** B4
Caister Avenue **8** F1
Calder Close **16** G2
Calder Road **7** B4
Caldy Avenue **11** C3
Cales Avenue **21** C3
Calgary Drive................**10** F2
Camberwell Drive **11** C3
Cambrai Drive **11** C4
Cambria Road **20** E1
Cambridge Close...........**26** F5
Camden Place................**6** H3
Cameron Court **24** E3
Camp Furlong **16** F2
Camp Hill (Droitwich)....**16** F2
Camp Hill (Gt. Malvern)..**21** A6
Camp Hill Avenue **7** B6
Camp Hill Road **7** B6
Camp Lane **1** D3
Campion Drive **24** G3
Canada Way **10** F2
Canalside **6** H1
Cangle Lane **8** F2
Cannon Street...............**11** C1
Canterbury Road............**7** D5
Carden Close **30** H4
Carden Court*, Carden Close
....................................**30** H4
Carden Street **30** H4

Carisbrooke Avenue **8** G1
Carlisle Road.................**7** D5
Carlton Road **21** D4
Carnforth Drive **7** D1
Carp Close **11** A4
Carriage Close................**6** F4
Carrock Fell **8** E2
Carters Close **7** C1
Cartmel Close **8** E1
Cartwright Avenue **8** F3
Castell Place **4** F6
Castle Close (Tenbury Wells)
....................................**29** C3
Castle Close (Worcester) **2** H5
Castle Place **30** G5
Castle Street (City Centre)
....................................**30** E2
Castle Street (Evesham) **20** E2
Catalpa Close **21** D1
Catbrook **7** B1
Cathedral Plaza*,
     Lychgate Precinct ..**30** G4
Catherine Road **10** E1
Causeway Lane **27** C3
Cavendish Street...........**11** A1
Cecil Road......................**7** A5
Cecilia Avenue **6** E1
Cecilia Place **6** E1
Cedar Avenue (Gt. Malvern)
....................................**22** E5
Cedar Avenue (Worcester)
....................................**7** C1
Cedar Close **16** G4
Cedar Cottages...............**1** D4
Cedar Court **17** A5
Cedars, The (Worcester)..**3** D2
Cedars, The*, Back La...**29** A2
Cedarwood Gardens **20** F3
Celandine Drive.............**11** A4
Celandine Way **19** D6
Celvestune Way **16** G3
Central Park **7** B5
Chacewater Avenue **2** G6
Chacewater Crescent **2** G6
Chadbury Road **17** B3
Chadwick **8** F3
Chaitley Villas **3** A4
Chalfont Close................**2** H6
Chalford Drive **3** D6
Challenger Close............**22** E6
Chalverton Court **16** F1
Chamberlain Court*,
     Bromsgrove Road ..**15** D5
Chamberlain Road..........**10** F1
Chance Lane **22** H6/**24** H1
Chantry Close **29** B4
Chantry House................**6** F5
Chapel Court*, Park St...**30** H4
Chapel Lane **15** A5
Chapel Mews.................**15** A5

Chapel Road **14** F4
Chapel Street (Badsey)..**17** A6
Chapel Street (Evesham)**20** E2
Chapel Walk **30** F4
Charity Crescent **20** E6
Charland Court **15** C2
Charlcote Mews **21** D6
Charlecot Road **16** F5
Charlemont*, Vimiera Close
....................................**11** D5
Charles Close **20** E4
Charles Dickens Close ..**16** G3
Charles Hastings Way......**8** E5
Charles Henry Road **15** D5
Charles Orchard **27** D4
Charles Street **30** G4/H4
Charles Way **22** F5
Charlock Road **24** G3
Charlotte Bronte Drive ..**16** G3
Charlton Close...............**19** B3
Charnwood Close **10** F2
Charter Place **30** E1
Chase End Close **11** C2
Chase Road..................**26** F5
Chatcombe Drive **3** D6
Chawson Lane **16** G1
Chawson Pleck **16** E2
Chawson Road **16** F3
Checketts Close (Pershore)
....................................**28** F1
Checketts Close (Worcester)
....................................**2** H6
Checketts Court **2** H5
Checketts Lane **2** H5
Chedworth Close............**4** E6
Chedworth Drive **4** E6
Chelmsford Court **7** D5
Chelmsford Drive **7** D5
Cheltenham Road (Broadway)
....................................**29** A2
Cheltenham Road (Evesham)
....................................**19** D4
Chepstow Avenue **8** F1
Chequers Close **22** G3
Chequers Lane (Worcester)
....................................**6** G4
Chequers Lane (Wychbold)
....................................**15** A6
Cherington Close **3** C6
Cherry Close (Droitwich) **16** F6
Cherry Close (Evesham)
....................................**20** G4
Cherry Close (Offenham)
....................................**18** G3
Cherry Orchard (Pershore)
....................................**28** G4
Cherry Orchard (Upton) **27** C3
Cherry Orchard House ..**28** G3
Cherry Street.................**11** A1
Cherry Tree Drive **23** D5

Cherry Tree Walk **30** F2
Cherwell Close **7** C3
Cherwell Court **7** C3
Cheshire Cheese Entry ..**30** F2
Chester Close **7** D5
Chester Place **21** C4
Chesterton Gardens **8** E4
Chestnut Close
     (Fernhill Heath) **3** D2
Chestnut Close (Hampton)
....................................**19** C4
Chestnut Court **24** F2
Chestnut Drive **23** D5
Chestnut Spinney **16** G4
Chestnut Street **6** H3
Chestnut Walk **6** H3
Chevenham Close..........**25** B2
Cheviot Close **7** C3
Childswickham Road......**29** A2
Chilham Place **4** F6
Chiltern Close **7** C3
Chorley Road **15** D4
Christ Church Road
     (Worcester)...............**7** B3
Christ Church Road
     (Gt. Malvern) **24** E2
Christina Close **14** F4
Christine Avenue.............**9** C1
Chub Close **11** A4
Church Close (Broadway)
....................................**29** B2
Church Close (Worcester) **6** F5
Church Cottages (Norton)
....................................**12** E6
Church Cottages (Upton)**27** B3
Church End **17** A6
Church Lane (Droitwich) **15** A6
Church Lane (Hallow) **1** D4
Church Lane
     (Lwr. Broadheath)......**1** A6
Church Lane
     (Martin Hussingtree)..**4** E1
Church Lane (Norton)
....................................**11** D5/**12** F5
Church Lane (Pinvin)......**28** F1
Church Lane (Whittington)
....................................**12** E3
Church Meadow Court ..**21** D6
Church Mews (Broadway)
....................................**29** B2
Church Mews (Tenbury Wells)
....................................**29** B4
Church Road (Droitwich)**15** D5
Church Road (Evesham)**19** C4
Church Road (Gt. Malvern)
....................................**21** D3
Church Road (Worcester)
....................................**7** B2
Church Street (Broadway)
....................................**29** A2

Church Street (City Centre)
...............................30 G3
Church Street (Evesham)
...............................20 E3
Church Street (Gt. Malvern)
...............................23 D1
Church Street (Kempsey)
...............................14 F4
Church Street (Offenham)
...............................18 G3
Church Street (Pershore)
...............................28 G5
Church Street (Tenbury Wells)
...............................29 B4
Church Street (Upton) 27 B3
Church Street (Wyre Piddle)
...............................28 H3
Church Terrace (Whittington)
...............................12 E3
Church Terrace (Worcester)
...............................6 F5
Church Walk (Gt. Malvern)
...............................23 D1
Church Walk (Norton) 18 E1
Church Walk (Pershore) 28 G5
Church Walk (Upton)....27 C3
Church Walk (Worcester)
...............................6 G5
Church Walk*, Church Street
...............................29 B4
Churchdown Road.......24 F4
Churchill Avenue 16 F3
Churchill Court 19 C4
Churchill Drive 22 F2
Cirencester Place 4 E6
City Arcade 30 G4
City Walls Road 30 G3
Claines Lane............2 H2/3 A3
Claphill Lane 5 B5/9 C1
Clare Road 22 F6
Clare Street....................30 H5
Clare Walk.....................21 D6
Claremount Court 26 E2
Clarence Close 24 E2
Clarence Road 23 D2/24 E2
Clarkes Hill House*,
    School Road............19 B3
Clarks Hill Rise 19 C3
Clarkson Gardens 8 F3
Claverham Close 10 G1
Clayfield Drive 21 C4
Clayhall Road 16 G5
Clayhill Cottages 1 C3
Clee Hill Road 29 B3
Clee View 16 F3
Cleeve Drive 7 D1
Clementi Court...............20 F2
Clerkenleap Cottages ...11 A5
Clerkenwell Crescent 21 D6
Clifford Close.................16 H3

Clifford Road 16 H3
Close Cottages*, Coppers La.
...............................20 E3
Clover Way 24 G3
Clyde Avenue 10 F3
Clydesdale Close 16 G6
Clydesdale Rise 16 G6
Clydesdale Road............16 G6
Cobden Avenue................8 F3
Coberley Close 3 D6
Cobham Court...............16 E4
Cobham Road 28 H1
Cockshot Road 21 D5/D6
Cockshute Hill 16 E4/E5
Coldicott Gardens 19 D4
Cole Hill...........................7 A5
Coleford Walk 16 G3
Colehurst Park*,
    Lansdowne Walk 7 A3
Coleridge Close 7 A1
Coleridge Court*, Kipling Cl.
...............................22 E6
Colesbourne Close 3 C6
Colford Close.................16 F1
Colin Road 2 G5
College Court 29 B5
College Gardens 29 B5
College Green (City Centre)
...............................30 G5
College Green (Droitwich)
...............................16 F3
College Grove 23 D3
College Precinct 30 G5
College Road 23 D3
College Street 30 G5
College Terrace*,
    Berrington Road 29 B5
College Yard 30 F5
Colletts Fields 29 C2
Colletts Gardens 29 C2
Colletts Green Road 9 B5
Collinghurst House*, New St.
...............................27 B3
Collings Avenue...............8 F4
Collinsfield 18 E6
Colman Road 15 D4
Coltishall Close 11 B3
Columbia Drive 10 E2
Columbine Grove 19 D6
Comer Avenue.................6 F4
Comer Gardens...............6 E3
Comer Road 6 F4
Commandery Court........30 H5
Commandery Road........30 G6
Common Road 20 E2
Como Road....................23 D1
Compton Road 7 B5
Conduit Hill 20 E2
Conduit House*, Rynal Place
...............................20 E2

Coney Green Close.........8 E1
Conisborough 4 F6/8 F1
Coniston Close (Gt. Malvern)
...............................24 G3
Coniston Close (Worcester)
...............................7 D2
Connaught Close...........11 B3
Conningsby Drive 28 E5
Constance Road 2 F5
Conway 7 D3
Conway Drive 20 G3
Coombs Road 2 H6
Coopers Close 7 D1
Coopers Lane 20 E3
Copcut Court 16 F2
Copcut Lane 16 H1
Cope Road 2 H6
Copenhagen Street 30 F4
Copper Croft 16 E4
Coppice Close (Droitwich)
...............................15 C2
Coppice Close (Gt. Malvern)
...............................21 C1
Coppice Close (Hallow)....1 D2
Coppice Way 15 C2
Copsewood Avenue 8 E4
Corbett Avenue 16 F4
Corbett House 16 E4
Corbett Street 16 E4
Corfe Avenue...................8 F1
Cormorant Rise 10 G2
Cornmarket 30 G3
Cornmarket Court*,
    Cornmarket 30 G3
Cornmeadow Green 2 H4
Cornmeadow Lane 2 H5
Cornmill Road 19 D5
Cornmore 28 E6/F6
Cornwall Gardens 29 B5
Coronation Avenue 9 B1
Coronation Road 22 F3
Coronation Street 20 F3
Corunna Close 11 C5
Cosgrove Close...............3 C5
Cotland 7 B1
Cotswold Court*, The Green
...............................29 B2
Cotswold Road 24 F1
Cotswold View 20 E2
Cotswold Way 3 D5
Cottage Row*, Gardens Walk
...............................27 B3
Cottages, The 1 B2
Council Houses
    (Chequers Lane) 15 A6
Council Houses (Crown East)
...............................5 A5
Council Houses
    (Worcester Road) ...15 A5
Court Cottages 18 G3

Court Gardens (Gt. Malvern)
...............................24 E2
Court Gardens (Kempsey)
...............................14 F4
Court Garth 14 F4
Court Lane 18 G3
Court Lea......................27 A5
Court Meadow 14 F4
Court Road 24 E3
Court Street...................27 B3
Court, The (Broadway) ..29 B2
Courtland Close 2 G4
Courtlands*, Bewdley Street
...............................19 D2
Cove Gardens..................2 G6
Coventry Arm Cottages ..10 E5
Coventry Avenue 10 G1
Coventry Homes*,
    The Holloway 15 D5
Coventry Terrace 28 G1
Cover Green 8 E3
Covercroft 15 D4
Cowl Barn Lane..............25 B1
Cowl Street 20 E2
Cowleigh Bank 21 B4
Cowleigh Court 21 B5
Cowleigh Park 21 B4
Cowleigh Road 21 A3/C5
Coxlea Close..................19 D1
Coxwell Drive.................22 F5
Crab Apple Way 20 F6
Cralves Mead 29 B4
Crane Drive...................10 G3
Cranesbill Drive 11 B4
Cranham Court 8 E1
Cranham Drive 3 D6
Craven Yard*, Church Street
...............................20 E3
Crescent Place 29 B6
Crescent Road 25 B2
Crescent Villas*, Kendall St.
...............................7 A3
Crescent, The (Colwall)..25 B2
Crescent, The (Gt. Malvern)
...............................26 F2
Crescent, The (Hindlip) 4 E3
Crescent, The (Tenbury Wells)
...............................29 B6
Cresswell Close 3 C3
Crickley Drive 3 D6
Cripplegate House*,
    St. Clements Close ..6 G5
Croft Bank 23 A1
Croft Farm Drive 23 A1
Croft Gardens 29 B2
Croft Road (City Centre) 30 E2
Croft Road (Evesham)....18 E6
Croft Walk 30 E3
Croftdown Court 23 C2
Crofters Close 15 B2

Crofters End 15 B2
Crofters Green...............15 B2
Crofters Hill...............15 B2
Crofters Way 15 B2
Cromwell Crescent 11 C1
Cromwell Crescent Lane 11 C1
Cromwell Road (Gt. Malvern)
...............................22 E4
Cromwell Road (Powick) 13 A1
Cromwell Street..............7 A4
Crookbarrow Road 11 C5
Crookbarrow Way 11 C4
Croome Road 10 F1
Cross Pool Cottages 2 H2
Cross Street 29 B5
Cross, The (City Centre) 30 G3
Cross, The (Offenham) ..18 H5
Cross, The (Upton) 27 B3
Crossley Road...............10 H1
Crosspool Cottages..........2 H2
Crown Chambers Court*,
    Friary Walk..............30 F3
Crown Close 1 A6
Crown Courtyard*, Bridge St.
...............................20 E2
Crown East Cottages..........5 A5
Crown East Lane..............5 A5
Crown Green Court 30 F1
Crown Lane 15 A5
Crown Lea Avenue 24 F2
Crown Lea Court 24 F2
Crown Meadow 1 A6
Crown Passage 30 F3
Crown Street 6 H1
Crown Walk*, Crown St. ..6 H1
Crowngate Centre 6 H4
Croydon Villas*, Oldbury Rd.
...............................6 E4
Crumpton Hill Road........21 A1
Crutch Lane 15 C5/D5
Cumberland Street...........6 H2
Cut Throat Lane 27 C1
Cuthbertson Court*,
    Highfield Close 16 E4
Cypress Close 20 F5
Cypress Street................6 H1
Cyril Road 7 A2

D

Dace Road 11 A4
Dalbury Close 21 D1
Dale, The........................16 E2
Dalegarth Court...............4 E6
Damaskfield.....................8 F3
Dancox House 6 G5
Danebury Park 21 B4
Danes Close 22 F4
Danes Green...................3 A3
Daniel House..................17 D6
Danube Close 16 G2

Dark Orchard..................29 B6
Dart Road 7 C4
Darwin Avenue 7 D4
Darwin Close.................14 G5
Dastons Close................29 C1
Daty Croft 8 E3
Davenham Close...........21 D6
Davies Road 19 D5/20 E5
Dawson Close 10 F2
De la Bere Close 20 E2
De Salis Court 15 A2
De Salis Drive 15 A2
De Waldon Road.............23 A2
De Wyche Bungalows 15 A6
De Wyche Close 15 A6
De Wyche Road 15 A6
Deacle Place 20 F2
Deal Crescent 4 G6
Dean Close 29 C3
Dean Park Cottages 29 B3
Deane Close.................13 A1
Deansway..............30 F3/F4
Debdale Avenue 8 F2
Deblins Green 13 A3
Dee Way 7 C3
Deer Avenue 11 C3
Deerhurst Terrace..........28 G1
Defford Road 28 E6/G6
Delamere Road 24 E1
Denison Close 22 F5
Dent Close 30 H4
Derby Road 30 H5
Dereham Court 21 D5
Derries, The 3 D2
Derwent Close................7 D1
Derwent Grove 16 F2
Devon Road 7 C6
Diana House*, Victoria Place
...............................7 A6
Dickinson Court 3 A6
Digby Road 20 F3
Diglis Avenue 6 H6
Diglis Court*, Diglis Rd.....6 H6
Diglis Dock Road...........10 H1
Diglis Lane....................11 A1
Diglis Road 6 H6
Dilmore Avenue...............3 C2
Dilmore Cottages.............3 B3
Dilmore Lane..................3 C3
Dinchall Road 12 E1
Dingle, The 23 A2
Dinmore Close...............11 B3
Dockeray Avenue 8 F2
Dodderhill Road............15 C2
Dogwood Close.............22 G5
Dolday.........................30 E3
Dolphin Close 6 F3
Don Road 7 C4
Donney Brook 20 F4
Dormouse Croft............11 C3

Dorothy Crescent 2 G4
Dorset House 16 E4
Dove Close 7 C4
Dovecote Road 16 F5
Dover Avenue 8 F1
Doverdale Close 16 E3
Doverdale Lane 15 A1
Doverdale Park Homes ..15 A2
Dowland Gardens 5 D4
Dowles Croft 15 D3
Downsland Cottages 25 B1
Dragonfly Green 11 C3
Drake Avenue 5 D4
Drakes Lea 20 F2
Drapers Close 3 C6
Draycote Close 11 B3
Drift, The 17 A5
Drive, The (Checketts Lane)
...............................2 H5
Drive, The (Elmdale Road)
...............................2 H5
Drive, The (Hindlip) 4 E3
Drive, The (Powick)..........9 B5
Droitwich Road
..2 H6/3 A5/B3/4 E2/6 H1
Drovers Green...............15 B3
Drovers Place 15 B3
Drovers Way (Droitwich) 15 B3
Drovers Way (Worcester)
...............................3 B6
Drumbles Lane 8 F2
Dryden Close (Gt. Malvern)
...............................22 E6
Dryden Close (Worcester)7 A1
Duck Meadow 8 E2
Dudley Close 5 D4
Dugard Way 16 H3
Dugdale Drive 8 F4
Duke of Edinburgh Way..22 F3
Dukes Way 24 F3
Dunkirk Drive...............11 D5
Dunmow Avenue 8 F4
Dunns Lane 27 B3
Dunster Close 4 F6
Durcott Lane 20 F3
Durcott Lodge*, Church St.
...............................20 E3
Durcott Road 20 E3
Durham Road 7 D4
Dutton Street 7 B3
Dyson Drive 24 G1

E

Eagle Close....................11 A4
Earlsdon Road................10 F1
East Bank Drive 2 G6
East Close 15 A6
East Comer 6 E3
East Park Drive 15 D2
East Street 30 G1

East Waterside 27 B3
Eastabrook Close 21 D3
Eastbury Cottages...........5 C1
Eastbury Manor Court......5 D1
Eastfield Close 3 C2
Eastnor Close 11 C2
Eastward Road 21 D2
Eastwick Drive...............19 D4
Easy Row 30 E1
Eaton Road 23 C6
Eatonhurst 24 F2
Ebrington Drive................4 E6
Ebrington Road 21 A6
Eden Court 11 A1
Edgar Street 30 G5
Edgehill Court*, Battenhall Wk.
...............................7 A6
Edgeworth Close 4 E6
Edith Berry Court............22 F6
Edith Walk.....................23 C1
Edmonton Close 10 F2
Edward Close 7 B6
Edward Elgar House*,
    Henwick Road 6 F3
Edward Hall House*,
    School Lane 27 C3
Edward Street 19 D2
Egg Lane 2 H1/3 A1
Egghill........................15 B3
Egremont Gardens 8 F2
Elbury Park Road 7 D3
Elgar Avenue 22 F5/G6
Elgar Court 7 A3
Elgar Crescent 16 G4
Elgar Drive 14 G5
Eliot Road 3 A6
Elizabeth Avenue (Droitwich)
...............................16 E5
Elizabeth Avenue (Worcester)
...............................2 H4
Elizabeth Court 16 E5
Elizabeth Road 20 E4
Elkstone Close 3 C6
Elliot Court 22 E5
Ellis Road 6 G6
Ellison Avenue.................6 E2
Ellsdon 14 G4
Ellsdon Rise 14 G4
Elm Court 11 A3
Elm Green Close 11 A3
Elm Road (Evesham) 20 F3
Elm Road (Worcester) 6 F4
Elm Villas.....................27 A5
Elmdale Road 2 H5
Elmfield Gardens.............7 B6
Elmley Close 24 F1
Elms Drive 25 A4
Elmside 20 F3
Eltric Road......................2 H5
Ely Close 7 D5

Emerald Road....

Emerald Road **6** E4
Emes Close **28** E5
Emperor Drive **11** C3
Engadine Close **24** E4
Enid Blyton Corner **16** G3
Ennerdale Close **7** D2
Enterprise Way **20** F6
Epsom Close **3** C2
Eskdale Close **7** D2
Essex Close (Collett's Green)
...................................**13** A1
Essex Close (Worcester)..**5** D5
Essex Drive **3** B3
Eston Avenue **24** G2
Evendene Road **19** B3
Evendine Close **11** B1
Evendine Corner **25** A4
Evendine Lane **25** A4
Everard Close **6** E2
Everard Place **6** E2
Eversley Close **22** E6
Eversley Grove **22** E5
Evesham Bypass
......**18** F4/**19** D6/**20** F6/H1
Evesham Road (Norton) **18** E3
Evesham Road (Offenham)
...................................**18** H6
Evesham Road*, Station Rd.
...................................**29** A1
Exbury Place..................**11** C3
Exeter Road **7** D4
Express Buildings*,
Howsell Road **21** D4

F

Fabricius Avenue **16** E4
Fairbairn Avenue.............**2** H5
Fairfax Court **6** G5
Fairfield Close **7** D1
Fairfield Place **19** D4
Fairfield Road **19** D4
Fairmont Close*, Fairmont Rd.
...................................**7** C1
Fairmont Road **7** C1
Fairoak Gardens **21** D6
Fairwater Close **20** E3
Fairway, The **7** D3
Fairways **28** G4
Fairways Walk **28** G4
Falcon Close (Droitwich) **16** G6
Falcon Close (Worcester)
...................................**11** A4
Falkland Road **20** F4
Fallow Field **8** F2
Falmouth **8** G1
Falstaff Drive.................**16** G3
Farleigh Road **28** F6
Farley Road....................**22** E3
Farley Street **6** E3
Farlie Close **14** F4

Farm Close **3** B6
Farmbank Road.............**15** A1
Farmbrook Close.............**5** D6
Farmers Court **15** C2
Farmers Green **15** C2
Farmers Piece................**15** C2
Farmers Way..................**15** C2
Farncombe Terrace **28** F6
Farne Avenue **11** C3
Farnham Green **8** F1
Farrier Street **30** F2
Farriers Close **15** C2
Farriers Corner **15** D2
Farriers Square **15** C2
Farriers Way **15** C2
Farrington House*, Bourne Cl.
...................................**16** E4
Farrington*, Vimiera Close
...................................**11** D5
Farundles Avenue **8** E2
Fearnal Close **3** D3
Fels Avenue.....................**8** F4
Fern Cottages **3** D2
Fern Road **6** E3
Fern Villas*, Droitwich Road
...................................**3** D2
Ferndale Close **2** G4
Fernhill Grove **24** E1
Ferry Bank **6** F2
Ferry Close **6** F2
Ferry Lane......................**18** G4
Ferry View **19** D3
Ferry Villas*, Park Av. **6** G1
Field Close (Worcester)....**7** B1
Field House Gardens*,
Wylds Lane **30** H5
Field Road **3** B6
Field Row*, Gardens Walk
...................................**27** B3
Field Walk **11** A2
Fielden Close **20** E3
Fielden Row....................**8** F4
Fieldfare Close **21** B2
Fieldhead Close **5** D6
Fields Close (Badsey) **17** B6
Finch Close **3** B2
Fir Tree Road **3** D2
Fir Tree Walk **22** E4
Fir Way **7** C1
Firlands Close **3** D2
Firlea*, School Lane **27** C3
Firs Close **23** D3
Firs Cottages.................**12** G5
Firs, The (Droitwich) **16** E2
Firs, The (Kempsey) **14** G3
First Avenue **10** G2
Fish Hill **29** D2
Fish Street.....................**30** G4
Fiskin Lane **8** F4
Fitcher Close **2** E6

Fitzwilliam Close **5** D4
Five Oaks Close **24** G1
Flag Meadow Walk **6** H2
Flats, The.......................**28** F6
Fleece Road **29** B1
Fleet Row **11** C3
Fleetwood Avenue.........**13** A1
Florence Avenue **16** F3
Florence Close.................**4** G5
Foley Road **10** F1
Foley Terrace **23** C2
Foley Walk **10** F1
Ford Close **24** G1
Fordbank Court **6** F2
Foregate Street **30** F1
Foregate, The **30** F2
Forest Close **6** E3
Forest Gate **20** E5
Forest, The **15** A2
Forresters Road **29** C3
Fort Royal Court **7** B6
Fort Royal Hill **30** H5
Fort Royal House **30** H5
Fort Royal Lane **7** A6
Fort Royal Mews **30** H6
Fossil Bank **23** B6
Fossil Bank Cottages **23** B6
Foster Road...................**20** E4
Fotheringhay **8** G1
Foundry Alley **30** H4
Foundry Street **30** H4
Fountain Court **19** D4
Fountain Gardens **19** D4
Fountain Place **6** G2
Four Pools Lane.........**20** E4/F5
Four Pools Road **20** E4
Fowler Avenue.................**8** F4
Fox Drive........................**11** C3
Foxes Hill **14** G4
Foxglove Close (Evesham)
...................................**20** F5
Foxglove Close (Gt. Malvern)
...................................**24** G3
Foxglove Road **11** A4
Foxhunter Close **16** G6
Foxwell Street **11** C1
Framlingham Close **11** B3
Franklin Close **10** F2
Fraser Close **24** E2
Frederick Road **21** D4
Freemantle Drive **14** G5
French Close **28** F4
Frenchlands Lane **1** A6
Friar Court*, Friar St......**30** G5
Friar Street (City Centre)
...................................**30** G5
Friar Street (Droitwich) ..**15** D4
Friary Square*, Friary Walk
...................................**30** F3
Friary Walk **30** F3

Fridays Acre **16** F2
Friends Cottages*,
The Foregate **30** G2
Friends Mews **30** G2
Friesland Close **3** B6
Frome Cottages.............**25** A4
Fruitlands **23** C5
Fry Close **8** F4
Fulbert Road **28** F6
Furlong, The **15** B3
Furlongs Road (Pershore)
...................................**28** G3
Furlongs Road (Upton) ..**27** C3
Furness Close **7** D2

G

Gallipoli Drive **11** C5
Galton Way **16** E6
Gamekeepers Drive **7** D1
Ganderton Court **28** G5
Garden Stiles **28** F5
Gardeners Close **7** C1
Gardens Close **27** C3
Gardens Walk **27** B3
Gardens, The **20** E1
Gardners Square*, Church St.
...................................**20** E3
Gawtree Way **8** F2
Gazala Drive **8** G1
Geneva Avenue.............**24** E4
Geneva Close **2** G5
Gentian Close **3** B2
Geoffrey Chaucer Walk..**16** G3
George Bayliss Road **15** C3
George Street (City Centre)
...................................**30** H3
George Street (Evesham)
...................................**19** D2
Georgina Avenue **10** G1
Geraldine Close **24** F3
Geraldine Court **24** F3
Geraldine Road **24** F2
Gheluvelt Court*, Brook St.
...................................**6** H2
Gibbs Lane **18** G3
Gibson Grove **21** C5
Giffard Drive **26** H6
Gig Bridge Lane............**28** F4
Gilbert Road **24** E1
Gillam Street **7** A2
Gilmour Crescent **2** H5
Glade, The (Gt. Malvern)
...................................**24** G1
Glade, The (Kempsey) ..**14** F3
Glebe Close.....................**6** F5
Glencoe Road **20** F2
Glendale **16** F2
Glenridding Close **8** E2
Glenthorne Avenue **7** C2
Gloucester Close **22** F2

Gloucester Court*,
Gloucester Close **22** F2
Gloucester Drive **13** A6
Gloucester Road **27** D1
Goddard Road.................**6** H2
Godsons Close **29** C4
Godsons Walk...............**29** C5
Golden Lion Arcade **30** G3
Goldsmith Road **7** C1
Goodalls Grove **19** D1
Goodrest Close **7** A2
Goodrest Walk................**7** A2
Goodrich Avenue..............**8** F1
Goodson Road **22** F3
Goodwood Avenue **11** B1
Goodwood Close (Evesham)
....................................**19** D5
Goodwood Close
(Fernhill Heath) **3** C3
Goodwood Close (Worcester)
....................................**11** B1
Goodwood Green **3** C3
Goodwood Road (Gt. Malvern)
....................................**22** E3
Goodwood Road (Pershore)
....................................**28** H1
Gordon Close **29** B2
Gordon Terrace..............**23** C5
Gorse Close **16** G5
Gorse Hill Road................**7** C2
Grafson Place **16** F2
Grafton Close **21** C5
Graftons, The **27** D4
Graham Court **21** D6
Graham Road (Gt. Malvern)
....................................**21** D5
Graham Road (Worcester)
....................................**6** F6
Grand Stand Road **6** G4
Grange Avenue **2** G4
Grange Cottages, The......**3** B2
Grange Lane (Fernhill Heath)
....................................**3** B3
Grange Lane (Rushwick)..**9** B1
Grange Road (Gt. Malvern)
....................................**23** D1
Grange Road
(Lwr. Broadheath)......**1** A6
Grange Way **8** G4
Grantham House*,
Salwarpe Road...........**15** D3
Grape Terrace*, Church St.
....................................**29** B4
Grasmere Drive...............**7** D2
Grasshopper Avenue **11** C3
Grassington Drive **8** E2
Grassy Bank **29** B6
Grayling Close................**11** A4
Great Calcroft **28** G6
Great Oaty Gardens **8** E2

Greathouse Road **6** F6
Green Close **25** A5
Green Field Close **8** E3
Green Hill Bath Road **30** H6
Green Hill London Road
....................................**30** H6
Green Hill Place **30** H6
Green Lane (Bevere) **2** G3
Green Lane (Gt. Malvern)
....................................**26** E2
Green Lane (Lwr. Broadheath)
............................**1** A6/B6
Green Lane (Upton) **27** B6
Green Lane (Worcester) ..**7** A2
Green Leys **17** A5
Green Street **14** H4
Green Valley Path **23** B1
Green, The (Broadway)..**29** B2
Green, The (Hallow) **1** D4
Green, The (Pinvin) **28** F1
Greenacres Road **6** E5
Greenbank....................**16** F6
Greenfield Close **8** E3
Greenfield Path **21** C6
Greenfields **27** C1
Greenfields Road **21** D3
Greenford Gardens **6** F2
Greenhill **18** E4
Greenhill Close **29** B4
Greenhill Cottages **1** D3
Greenhill Drive..............**24** E1
Greenhill Gardens **29** B5
Greenhill Lane................**1** D3
Greenhill Park Road..**18** E5/E6
Greenhill Terrace............**18** E6
Greenway, The **9** C5
Gregorys Bank **6** H2
Gregorys Court **6** H2
Gregorys Mill Street **6** H1
Grenville Road **5** D5
Gresham Court*,
Shrubbery Avenue **6** H2
Gresham Road **5** D4
Gresley Road **4** E6
Grisedale Drive **8** E1
Grit Lane **21** C1
Grosmont Avenue **8** G1
Grosvenor Close **16** G6
Grosvenor Crescent **16** F5
Grosvenor Walk..............**6** F5
Grosvenor Way **16** F5
Grove Cottages (Upton) **27** B6
Grove Cottages*,
Bromyard Road **5** D5
Grove Cottages*, Church La.
....................................**12** E3
Grove Crescent (Upton) **27** B6
Grove Crescent (Worcester)
....................................**5** D5
Grove Field **4** E6

Grove Way **9** D1
Grove, The (Upton) **27** B6
Grove, The (Worcester) ..**2** H4
Grovewood Road **22** G3
Grundys Lane **26** E2
Guarlford Road **24** G2
Guildford Close **7** C5
Gurneys Lane **15** D5

H

Hadley Villas **3** A4
Hadzor Lane **16** E6
Haggs Meadow................**8** G2
Hailsham Close **11** B1
Haines Avenue **8** F4
Haines Place **19** D2
Haisley Row....................**8** F2
Halas House **26** E1
Hales Orchard.................**6** G6
Halfkey Court.................**21** B1
Halfkey Road.................**21** B1
Halifax Drive **10** F2
Hall Close **8** E2
Hall Green (Gt. Malvern) **24** H2
Hall Green (Upton) **27** D4
Hall Green Close.............**24** H2
Hallow Lane....................**1** A6
Hallow Park **2** E4
Hallow Road **2** E6/**6** E1
Ham Lane **9** C5
Ham View **27** C3
Hamble Close **7** C5
Hamilton Close **9** C6
Hamilton Road (City Centre)
....................................**30** H5
Hamilton Road (Evesham)
....................................**19** D4
Hamilton Square **30** E1
Hammond Close **16** G5
Hammond Court*, Galton Way
....................................**16** E6
Hampden Road **22** E4
Hampton Close **6** E4
Hampton Gardens **6** F4
Hampton House*, School Rd.
....................................**19** B3
Hampton Park **15** A2
Hampton Road **15** D4
Hams Way.......................**9** D1
Hanbury Avenue **10** F1
Hanbury Park Road........**10** F1
Hanbury Road................**15** D5
Hanbury Street **15** D5
Hanbury Wharf*, Hanbury Rd.
....................................**15** D5
Hancocks Lane **26** F6
Handbury Road **22** E3
Hanley Road (Gt. Malvern)
....................................**26** E2
Hanley Road (Upton)......**27** A1

Hanley Terrace **23** C6
Hanover Court*, Elkstone Ct.
....**3** C6
Hanson Way **28** F6
Happy Land North **6** F5
Happy Land West **6** F5
Happy Valley **23** C1
Harbinger Avenue **22** F6
Harbour Drive **25** B1
Harcourt Road.................**23** A2
Harden Court*, Thorneloe Wk.
....**6** G2
Hardings Court **28** F5
Hardknott Row **8** G1
Hardwick Terrace*,
Walwyn Road **25** B2
Hardwicke Close **6** F4
Hardy Court.....................**6** H1
Haresfield Close **3** D6
Harlech Close **8** F1
Harrington Road **5** D5
Harris Close...................**16** E3
Harris Hill*, Union Lane..**15** D4
Harrison Close...............**13** A1
Harrow Croft **5** D6
Harter Row **7** D1
Hartwell House*, Mill Street
....................................**20** E2
Harvey Road **20** F2
Harvey Walk **7** A2
Haselor Lane **19** A4
Hastings Drive **8** F1
Hastings Road **24** G2
Hatfield Lane **12** E6
Hathaway Close **5** D4
Hawford House **2** H1
Hawford Lock Lane **2** G1
Hawford Place **16** F2
Hawkesbury House*, Mill St.
....................................**20** E2
Hawkins Close **5** D4
Hawkley Row...................**8** F2
Hawkshead Court **8** E1
Hawkwood Close **21** C4
Hawkwood Crescent **6** E3
Hawthorn Lane **24** F5
Hawthorn Road (Evesham)
....................................**20** F4
Hawthorn Road (Worcester)
....**7** B3
Hawthorn Walk **16** G4
Hay Close **8** E3
Hayes Bank Road **24** F4
Hayfield Close **5** D6
Hayling Close **11** C3
Haynes Court **22** E3
Haysfield, The **22** F4
Hayslan Avenue **22** E6
Hayslan Green **22** E6
Hayslan Road **22** F6

Haywain Avenue 8 F2
Haze Croft 8 F2
Hazel Avenue 20 F4
Hazel Close (Droitwich) 16 G4
Hazel Close (Worcester) ..7 C2
Hazelwood Close 7 D6
Head Street 28 F5
Heath Close 1 D2
Heath Drive 11 C4
Heath Terrace 1 D2
Heather Close 11 A4
Heathers, The 19 D6
Heathfield Road..............18 E1
Heathlands 28 G4
Heathlands Close 26 F4
Hebb Street 6 H3
Heights, The 8 E4
Helford Close 7 C5
Hemmingway...................20 E4
Hemsby Close 11 B3
Hemsley Place.................8 F1
Henley Drive 16 G5
Henley Place 21 C5
Henry Fowler Close........19 D1
Henry Street (Evesham) 19 D2
Henry Street (Worcester)..6 H2
Henwick Avenue 6 F4
Henwick Court.................6 G5
Henwick House*,
    St. Clements Close ..6 G5
Henwick Parade 6 F3
Henwick Road 6 F2/F3
Herefordshire House*,
    Bransford Road 6 F6
Heriotts Court 15 D5
Heriotts Lane 15 D5
Heriotts, The 16 E5
Heritage Way..................16 E4
Herne Field 8 F2
Heron Close 10 G2
Heron Place 15 D6
Hetherington Close 14 F3
Hetherington Rise 8 F4
Hever Avenue 8 F1
Heywell Walk..................23 C2
Hidcote Close 11 B3
High Park 12 G5
High Street (Badsey)......17 A5
High Street (Broadway) ..29 B2
High Street (City Centre)30 G3
High Street (Evesham) ..19 D2
High Street (Pershore) ..28 G4
High Street (Upton) 27 B3
Highfield 13 D3
Highfield Close (Droitwich)
    ....16 E4
Highfield Close (Gt. Malvern)
    ....21 D4
Highfield Road (Evesham)
    ....19 B2/B3

Highfield Road (Gt. Malvern)
    ....21 D4
Highgate Court 29 A2
Highland Road................7 B2
Hill Avenue, The 7 A6/11 A1
Hill Close 28 F5
Hill Street 7 A4
Hill View Close (Colwall) 25 B1
Hill View Close (Gt. Malvern)
    ....22 F3
Hill View Gardens 27 B5
Hill View Road 10 F1
Hill Walk 21 D6
Hill Wood Close 8 F2
Hillcrest 20 G4
Hillcrest Rise 2 G4
Hillend 15 D6
Hillery Road.....................7 C6
Hillsfield 27 C3
Hillside 14 G3
Hillside Close (Hampton)
    ....19 B3
Hillside Close (Worcester)
    ....7 C4
Hillstone Court...............23 D1
Hillview Drive.................21 C4
Hilton Road 24 G3
Himbleton House*,
    Himbleton Road 6 E2
Himbleton Road...............6 E2
Hindlip Lane 3 B4/D4/4 E4
Hingley Avenue 8 F3
Hipkiss Gardens 15 C3
Hither Green 17 A5
Hobhouse Gardens 8 F4
Hock Coppice 8 E3
Hodges, The 20 E2
Holdings Lane 14 H1/H2
Holland Drive...................7 B3
Holland Green 8 F3
Hollies Mews, The 22 F3
Holloway (Pershore) 28 E4
Holloway Drive 28 E4
Holloway, The (Droitwich)
    ....15 D5
Holly Close (Droitwich) ..16 G5
Holly Close (Evesham) ..20 F4
Holly Road 29 B3
Holly Tree Lane................9 C1
Hollygrove 27 A5
Hollymount 7 C3
Hollymount Road..............7 C2
Holmwood Gardens........20 F5
Holyoake Cottages*,
    Defford Road 28 G6
Holyrood Apartments 23 C1
Holywell Hill 6 F4
Holywell Mews.................26 E3
Holywell Road.................26 E1
Home Piece...................16 E2

Homefield Road 6 G6
Homenash House*,
    St. Georges Lane North
    ....6 H2
Homesmith House*,
    St. Marys Road........20 E1
Homestead 16 F3
Homestead Avenue.........4 E6
Homestead Close 26 E4
Homeward Bound 22 E5
Honeymans Gardens 15 C3
Honeysuckle Close 19 D6
Honeywood Road 6 E3
Honister Drive 8 E1
Hood Street*, Quay St. ..30 F4
Hop Kiln, The 29 D5
Hop Warehouse, The 30 G1
Hope Court*, Checketts Lane
    ....2 H5
Hopkiln Gardens 19 D2
Hopmarket The*,
    St. Nicholas Street ..30 G3
Hopton Street 6 F5
Hornsby Avenue 8 F3
Hornyold Avenue............21 C5
Hornyold Court 26 E1
Hornyold Road 21 C5
Horsebridge Avenue 17 A4
Horsford Road 6 F2
Hoskyns Avenue 8 F4
Hospital Bank 21 C4
Hospital Lane 9 C6
Hospital Road 21 B2
Howard Road 5 C4
Howcroft Green 8 E1
Howells Road 21 D4
Howlett Place 8 G4
Howsells, The 22 F2
Hudson Close (Pershore)
    ....28 F4
Hudson Close (Worcester)
    ....10 F2
Humber Road 7 C4
Hungerpit Walk.................2 H6
Hunstanton Close 11 B3
Hunt Avenue 8 F3
Hunter Rise 28 E5
Hunters Close 15 C2
Hunters End 15 D2
Hunters Green................15 D2
Hunters Place 15 D2
Hunters Way 15 D2
Huntings, The 29 B2
Hurst Lane.......................3 D3
Hurst Park Cottages 28 G2
Hurst Road 28 G3
Huxleys Way 19 D2
Huxtable Rise 8 F3
Hyacinth Close 11 A4
Hyde Lane.......................27 C1

Hydefields 27 C1
Hydrangea Close............11 A4
Hylton Parade 30 E4
Hylton Road (Hampton)..19 B3
Hylton Road (Worcester)..6 F3

I

Ideleton 8 F4
Ilkley Close 7 D3
Imperial Road 24 E1
Impney Green 15 D6
Impney Walk 15 D6
Inches Lane 20 E1
Inett Way 15 D1
Infirmary Walk 30 F2
Ingles Drive 6 F5
Inglethorpe Court*,
    Sansome Street 30 G3
Ingrams Barn*, Main Street
    ....18 H4
Isaac Walk 6 E6
Isaacs Way 16 H4
Isbourne Crescent..........19 D4
Iverley Court 29 C3
Ivy Court 20 F2
Ivy Lane...........................3 D3
Ivy Street.........................6 G1

J

Jackdaw Lane 16 H6
Jacob Close.....................3 B6
Jacobs Ladder Lane 3 B1
Jacomb Close 1 A6
Jacomb Drive 1 A6
Jakemans Hill Cottages..15 A2
Jamaica Crescent 21 D3
Jamaica Road 21 D3
James Close 30 H3
Jasmine Close 11 B4
Jasmine Road 23 C5
Jasmine Walk 19 D5
Jasper Road 10 F2
Jennet Tree Lane
    ....13 A4/22 H6
Jenny Lind Grove 21 D5
John Comyn Drive............3 A5
John Gwynn House*,
    Newport Street 30 E3
John Martin Square........19 C4
Joiners Close 7 C1
Jubilee Drive 25 C6
Jubilee Road 10 G1
Jubilee Villas*, The Cross
    ....18 H5
Judge Court....................15 B3
Juniper Way 23 C6

K

Keats Avenue 7 A1
Keble Close 7 B4

Keephill Cottages*,
  Droitwich Road.........3 D2
Keil Close 29 B2
Kempton Close 19 C4/D4
Kempton Road 28 H2
Kendal Green 8 E1
Kendal Street....................7 A3
Kenilworth Close 7 A3
Kenilworth Court 30 H1
Kennel Cottages 3 D1
Kennel Lane (Broadway)
  ....29 B2
Kennels Lane (Fernhill Heath)
  ....3 C1
Kennet Green 7 B5
Kensington Mews 21 D6
Kent Close (Evesham) ..19 B3
Kent Close (Gt. Malvern)22 F2
Kentmere Close 7 D2
Kents Green 13 B3
Kenwood Avenue 7 C3
Kenwood Close 7 D3
Kepax Gardens................6 G1
Keren Drive 11 D5
Kerry Hill 3 C5
Kestrel Crescent 16 H6
Kestrel Drive 11 A4
Keswick Drive 7 D1
Ketch Caravan Park 11 A5
Key Avenue 8 F4
Kidderminster Road ..15 A2/B2
Kielder Rise 10 F2
Kilbury Drive 12 E1
King Arthurs Close...........6 F3
King Charles Avenue 9 C6
King Charles Court*, Bath Rd.
  ....30 H6
King Charles Court*, Vine St.
  ....19 D2
King Charles Place*, St. Johns
  ....6 F6
King Edmunds Square ..30 E1
King Edwards Road 23 C5
King Georges Way 28 G5
King Johns Square 30 E1
King Stephens Mount 6 F2
King Street 30 G5
Kingfisher Close 11 B3
Kingfisher Court*, Waterside
  ....15 D5
Kings Court (Droitwich) ..15 D5
Kings Court (Eveham) 20 F2
Kings End Road.........9 B5/D5
Kings Hill.......................14 G2
Kings Lane 17 D1
Kings Road (Evesham) .20 F3
Kings Road (Gt. Malvern)
  ....26 E4
Kingsbury Road 10 F1
Kingsdale Court.............29 C2

Kingshill Close...............24 E1
Kingston Close 16 G5
Kingston Avenue 7 A1
Kingswood Road 15 A1
Kinnersley Road 21 C2
Kinord Close 11 C2
Kipling Close (Gt. Malvern)
  ....22 E6
Kipling Close (Worcester) 7 A1
Kirkby Gardens 7 D1
Kirkham House 3 A5
Kirkstone Drive 7 D2
Kleve Walk.....................30 F5
Knapp Place 11 B3
Knapp Way 21 D3
Knapp, The 17 A6
Knight Street 6 F5
Knoll Lane 24 F4
Knotts Avenue 8 F2
Knowle Hill.....................20 F4
Knowledge Cottages......18 G4
Kohima Drive.................11 C5
Kyreside 29 B5
Kyrewood Court 29 D5
Kyrewood Road.............29 C4

L

Labrador Road...............10 F3
Laburnum Cottages 18 G4
Laburnum Drive 20 F5
Laburnum Road 7 C3
Laburnum Walk (Gt. Malvern)
  ....21 C5
Laburnum Walk (Upton) 27 C3
Lady Howard de Warden Drive
  ....23 B1
Ladygo Lane 1 D3
Lahn Drive.....................16 G2
Lamb Bank 21 B5
Lambert Court*, Lambert Rd.
  ....6 F5
Lambert Road 6 F5
Lambourne Avenue........22 E3
Lambourne Crescent........6 E1
Lancaster Close 27 C4
Lancelott Court 28 F4
Lancing Close 11 B1
Lane House*, Eastfield Close
  ....3 C2
Lanes End 14 F4
Lanesfield Park 18 E6
Langdale Close 7 D1
Langdale Drive 7 D1/D2
Langdale Road 6 G2
Langland Avenue...........22 F6
Langland Close 24 F1
Langley Close 6 E2
Langley Road 16 F5
Lankets, The 17 A5
Lansdowne Close 24 F1

Lansdowne Court (Evesham)
  ....20 F3
Lansdowne Court*,
  Lansdowne Road 6 H3
Lansdowne Crescent
  (Gt. Malvern) 24 E1
Lansdowne Crescent
  (Worcester)...............7 A3
Lansdowne Crescent Lane
  ....7 A2
Lansdowne House*,
  Madresfield Road 24 E1
Lansdowne House*, Port St.
  ....20 F3
Lansdowne Mews (Worcester)
  ....7 A2
Lansdowne Mews*, Port St.
  ....20 F3
Lansdowne Rise 7 A2
Lansdowne Road
  (Gt. Malvern) 21 D4
Lansdowne Road (Worcester)
  ....6 H3
Lansdowne Row 24 E1
Lansdowne Street 6 H2
Lansdowne Terrace
  (Gt. Malvern) 24 E1
Lansdowne Terrace
  (Worcester) 6 H2
Lansdowne Walk 7 A3
Lapal Close 6 F5
Larch Road (Evesham) ..20 F5
Larch Road (Worcester) ..7 B3
Larches, The 16 E4
Larchfield Close 21 C4
Lark Hill 7 C6
Lark Hill Road 7 B6
Larkspur Drive...............19 D5
Larkspur House...............2 G4
Larkspur Road...............11 B4
Laslett Street 7 A2
Lasletts Almshouses*,
  Union Street 30 G4
Laugherne Road 6 F4
Launceston Place 8 F1
Laurel Avenue 20 F4
Laurel Road (Worcester)..7 C2
Laurels Road (Offenham)
  ....18 H5
Laurelwood Close 16 G6
Laurelwood Road 16 G5
Lavender Road 6 G1
Lavender Walk (Evesham)
  ....19 D6
Lavender Walk (Gt. Malvern)
  ....24 G3
Lawns, The 14 G5
Lawnside Close..............27 C1
Lawson Gardens...........27 C4
Laxton Avenue 6 E1

Layland Walk.................10 H1
Laylocks Lane 5 A3
Layton Avenue...............22 F5
Lea Close 2 H4
Leabank Drive..................2 G4
Leadon Road.................24 H2
Leahill Close 21 D5
Leamington Court 26 E3
Leamington Road 29 C1
Lear Close 5 D4
Leas Almshouses 30 F3
Leasowe Close 5 D6
Leasowes Road 18 H4
Lechmere Crescent
  (Gt. Malvern) 21 D3
Lechmere Crescent
  (Worcester)...............6 E2
Leckhampton Close 3 D6
Ledwych Close 15 D3
Ledwych Gardens 16 E3
Ledwych Road 15 D3
Leeds Avenue 8 F1
Lees, The 23 D3
Leicester Grove 20 E2
Leicester Street...............6 G2
Leigh Grove...................15 D3
Leigh Sinton Road 21 C2/C3
Leopard Rise 8 E4
Leslie Avenue 2 G4
Leven Drive 11 C3
Lewes Gardens 8 F1
Leycroft 16 F6
Leys Walk 20 E2
Leys, The (Claines) 3 B1
Leys, The (Evesham) 20 E2
Lichfield Avenue (Evesham)
  ....20 F2
Lichfield Avenue (Worcester)
  ....7 D4
Lifford Gardens 29 A2
Lilac Avenue 7 B3
Lilac Close (Droitwich) ..16 G6
Lilac Close (Eveham) ...19 B4
Lilac Close (Upton) 27 C3
Lilac Cottages 5 B1
Lime Avenue 7 C1
Lime Street 20 F2/F3
Lime Tree Avenue (Broadway)
  ....29 C1
Lime Tree Avenue
  (Gt. Malvern) 23 C6
Limes, The 14 G3
Lincoln Green 7 D5
Linden Close 20 F5
Linden Road 7 C2
Lindsey Avenue 20 F3
Lineage Cottages 29 A3
Lineage Court 29 B3
Lingfield Road 19 C4
Lingmell Court 8 E1

Link Elm Close...............10 F2
Link Road 20 E5
Link Terrace 21 D5
Link Way 22 E4
Linksview Crescent 8 E4
Linley Close 2 G4
Lion Court 30 G2
Lion Walk 30 H1
Lismore Green 11 C3
Lister Avenue..................8 F4
Little Broughton Walk 6 E6
Little Chestnut Street.......7 A3
Little Hill.......................16 F2
Little Hill Court...............16 E2
Little Hill Green 16 F1
Little London 6 H3
Little Orchard................16 F3
Little Park.....................16 F2
Little Penny Rope 28 F6
Little Piece......................8 F2
Little Priest Lane 28 G5
Little Southfield Street....30 G2
Littleworth Street...........19 D2
Littleworth Walk.............19 D2
Liverpool Road 7 C6
Livingstone Street 11 C1
Lloyd Close 18 E1
Lobelia Close................11 B4
Lock Cottages*,
    Diglis Dock Road 10 H1
Lock Street 30 H4
Lock View*, Mill Bank ...20 E2
Lodge Close 6 E3
Lodge Drive..................21 C6
Lodge Farm Cottages 9 A6
London Lane 27 B3
London Road 30 H6/11 D1
Long Bank 15 A3
Long Hedges 28 E6
Long Meadow 29 C3
Long Sling 16 F3
Longdon Court 20 H6
Longdon Hill 20 H6
Longfellow Road 6 H1
Longfield 27 C3
Longridge Road.............24 F4
Longthorpe 8 F1
Lords Heath 8 F2
Loughmill Road 28 F4
Loves Grove 30 F1
Lovett Place....................8 F3
Lovett Road 15 A2
Lovington Lane 1 B6/5 B1
Low Fold Close 5 D6
Lowell Street 30 H1
Lower Barbourne Terrace*,
    Selbourne Rd. West 6 G2
Lower Chase Road 24 F2
Lower Chestnut Street 6 H3
Lower Ferry Lane 13 D3

Lower Field Terrace 6 H6
Lower Green 29 A2
Lower Howsell Road 22 E1/F3
Lower Leys 20 E2
Lower Meadow 16 F3
Lower Mill Cottages........29 A2
Lower Montpelier Road ..23 A1
Lower Priest Lane 28 G5
Lower Quest Hills Road 21 D4
Lower Road 21 A6
Lower Town.....................3 C1
Lower Wilton Road 24 F1
Lower Wyche Road........23 C5
Lowesmoor 30 G2
Lowesmoor House*,
    Lowesmoor Terrace 30 H2
Lowesmoor Place 30 H2
Lowesmoor Terrace 30 H2
Lucerne Avenue 24 E4
Lucerne Close 2 F4
Ludlow Avenue 8 F1
Ludlow Road 29 C4
Ludstock Close 12 E1
Lugano Road 2 G5
Lullowfield House 16 E6
Lundy Row 11 C3
Lutterworth Close 7 D3
Lychgate 30 G4
Lychgate Precinct 30 G4
Lydes Road 24 F1
Lydford Terrace 8 F1
Lyfs Lane......................14 F4
Lygon Bank 21 D5
Lygon Lodge 22 G2
Lyneham Close 3 C6
Lynwood Close 19 B3
Lyttelton Court...............16 E5
Lyttelton Road 16 F4
Lyttleton Road 28 H1
Lyttleton Square 22 E3
Lyttleton Street 6 G2

Macauley Rise................22 E5
Machine Cottages*,
    Boraston Lane 29 B3
Madresfield Road
    ....22 G6/24 E1
Magdala Court*, The Butts
    ....30 F3
Magnolia Close 11 A4
Magpie Close 11 A4
Magpie Court*, Avon St. 19 D2
Main Road (Hallow)..........1 D1
Main Road (Kempsey) ..14 G4
Main Street (Offenham)
    ....18 G3/H4
Main Street (Pinvin) ..28 E2/F1
Malham Place 11 C2
Malins Hill Road 19 B3

Mallard Close 10 G2
Mallard Place 15 D6
Mallow Close.................24 G3
Malt House Mews 29 B4
Malthouse Place 30 F3
Malton Close 21 C2
Malus Close 22 G5
Malvern Close 1 A6
Malvern Gate 10 G2
Malvern Meadows
    Caravan Park 24 F6
Malvern Road
    ....6 F6/9 B6/10 F3
Malvern View 8 E4
Malvern Walk...................1 A6
Manby Road 24 E2
Mandalay Drive 11 C5
Manitoba Close 10 E3
Manning Place*, Sansome Pl.
    ....30 G2
Manning Road................16 E3
Manor Close (Badsey)....17 A5
Manor Close (Droitwich) 16 E5
Manor Farm Cottages*,
    Church Street 28 G5
Manor Gardens 28 G6
Manor Road 10 F1
Manorfield 1 B6
Manorside 17 A5
Mansfield Road 22 G4
Mansion Gardens 20 E3
Mapit Place 8 F3
Maple Avenue (Pershore)
    ....28 G4
Maple Avenue (Worcester)
    ....7 C3
Maple Close...................20 F4
Maple Grove 16 G4
Maple Road....................22 G4
Margaret Road 10 G1
Marhon Close 16 G6
Marigold Close 11 A4
Marion Close....................2 G5
Mark Close 21 C2
Market Gate 28 G5
Market Passage*, New Street
    ....30 G4
Market Place 19 D2
Market Square...............29 B4
Market Street.................29 B4
Marl Bank*, Lansdowne Walk
    ....7 A3
Marlbank Road 26 E6
Marlborough Gardens ...22 E2
Marlborough Street 11 C1
Marlow Court*, Britannia Sq.
    ....6 H3
Marlow Road..................5 D4
Marsh Avenue 8 E2
Marsh Close 22 F6

Marten Croft 11 C3
Martin Avenue 19 B4
Martin Close 22 G6
Martindale Close 8 E1
Martins Almshouses*,
    Defford Road 28 G6
Martins Orchard.............25 A3
Martley Road ..1 A6/5 B1/6 E2
Marymans Road 19 B4
Masefield Close...............2 H6
Mason Close 22 F5
Masons Court 20 F2
Masons Drive 3 C6
Masons Ryde 28 G5
Masons Way*, Bridge Street
    ....28 G5
Masters Close 20 F3
Mathon Road.................21 A6
Matravers Road 22 F6
Matthias Close...............22 E3
Maund Street...................6 E3
Mavis Cottages 13 C3
May Avenue 7 B3
May Tree Hill.................16 G5
Maybank 22 G5
Maycroft........................19 B4
Mayfair..........................20 E4
Mayfield Avenue 7 A2
Mayfield Road (Madresfield)
    ....22 G5
Mayfield Road (Pershore)
    ....28 G3
Mayfield Road (Worcester)
    ....7 A2
Mayflower Close 24 F1
Mayflower Road 16 E6
Maytree Hill 15 C2
McCormick Avenue 8 F4
McIntyre Road 6 F5
McKenzie Way 7 B4
McNaught Place 30 F1
Mead, The 6 E3
Meade Court*, Merstow Place
    ....19 D2
Meadow Close (Droitwich)
    ....15 C2
Meadow Close (Kempsey)
    ....14 F5
Meadow Court 15 C2
Meadow Green 15 C2
Meadow Orchard...........29 C2
Meadow Piece................15 C2
Meadow Place................15 C3
Meadow Rise 29 C3
Meadow Road (Droitwich)
    ....15 C2
Meadow Road (Gt. Malvern)
    ....22 E5
Meadow Road (Worcester)
    ....2 H3

Meadow Side..................27 B5
Meadow Sweet Court 24 G3
Meadow Sweet House*,
    Whinfield Gardens ..2 G4
Meadow Walk (Droitwich)
    ....15 C2
Meadow Walk (Pershore)
    ....28 G3
Meadow Way 15 C2
Meadowbank Drive 5 D5
Meadows End 19 B3
Meadows, The*, Eastfield Cl.
    ....3 C2
Meadway.......................21 D3
Mealcheapen Street 30 G3
Medina House 10 H1
Medway Road (Evesham)
    ....20 F3
Medway Road (Worcester)
    ....7 B5/C5
Melbourne Street.............6 H1
Melrose Close 6 F4
Melsungen Allee*, Bridge St.
    ....19 D2
Mendip Close (Gt. Malvern)
    ....24 F1
Mendip Close (Worcester)
    ....7 C3
Menston Close 8 E2
Mercia Drive 15 A2
Merebrook Close 26 F4
Merick Road 22 F3
Merrick House*,
    St. Clements Close ..6 G5
Merrimans Court 6 H2
Merrimans Hill Road 6 H2
Merrimans Walk 7 A2
Merrivale Court 24 F2
Merrybrook 19 B3
Mersey Road...................7 C4
Merstow Cottages*,
    Merstow Place 19 D2
Merstow Green 19 D2
Merstow Place...............19 D2
Merton Close...................7 C4
Merton Road 22 E3
Mews, The (Bevere) 2 G2
Mews, The (Gt. Malvern)
    ....26 E3
Mews, The (Pershore) 28 F5
Mews, The (Tenbury Wells)
    ....29 B4
Mews, The*, High St. ...19 D2
Michael Crescent 21 D2
Michael Tippett Drive.......7 B4
Middle Battenhall Cottages
    ....11 C2
Middle Hollow Drive.........8 E2
Middle Lane...................16 H6
Middle Road 6 F6

Middle Street..................30 G1
Middles Avenue...............8 E3
Middleton Gardens 8 E2
Midhurst Close 7 B6
Midland Road 7 B5
Midway Cottages*,
    Leamington Road 29 B1
Milestone Road 27 C1
Milestone, The 28 G6
Mill Avenue 29 A2
Mill Bank 20 E2
Mill Court 15 D3
Mill House Caravan Park 2 H1
Mill Lane (Badsey)..........17 A6
Mill Lane (Colwall) 25 A3
Mill Lane (Gt. Malvern) ..24 G4
Mill Lane (Offenham)......18 H5
Mill Lane (Pershore) 28 G3
Mill Lane (Wychbold)......15 A6
Mill Lane Close 28 G3
Mill Meadow 29 C6
Mill Road 19 C4
Mill Row Cottages 28 G3
Mill Stream Court...........20 E2
Mill Street (City Centre)..30 G6
Mill Street (Evesham) 20 E2
Mill Wood Drive 8 E3
Millbrook Close 2 G6
Millennium Way 20 F6
Miller Street 16 E4
Millers Close 7 C1
Millers Croft 24 G2
Millhams Avenue 8 F2
Mills Close 29 B1
Milret Close 7 A2
Milton Close....................7 A1
Milton Court*, Kipling Close
    ....22 E6
Minett Avenue 9 C1
Minge Lane 27 C3
Minter Avenue 16 E4
Moat Court 9 C5
Moat Crescent...............24 G1
Moat House Barns...........3 B4
Moat House Lane 3 B4
Moatway 24 G1
Monach Drive 6 E1
Monarch Place 6 E2
Monarchs Way 3 C1
Monks Close 28 G5
Monks Walk 20 E3
Monkswell Court 30 F3
Monnow Close (Droitwich)
    ....16 G3
Monnow Close (Gt. Malvern)
    ....24 H1
Monsell Lane.................27 D1
Montfort Street...............20 F2
Montgomerie Close 13 A1
Montpelier Road 23 A1

Montreal Close 10 F3
Moor House*, Armstrong Drive
    ....6 H6
Moor Street 30 E1
Moorings, The 30 H2
Moorlands Court 21 D5
Moorlands Road 21 D5
Moorlands, The 26 F2
Moors, The 30 E1
Moreland Road 16 E3
Moreton Place 30 F3
Morgan Court 21 D5
Morningside...................29 A5
Morrin Close 2 H4
Morris Avenue 2 H5
Morris Road 29 B1
Mortimers Quay 20 E2
Mortlake Avenue 7 C6
Morton Avenue 3 B3
Morton Road 3 B3
Mosel Drive 16 G2
Moseley Road 1 A1/B1
Mount Orchard 29 B5
Mount Pleasant (Pershore)
    ....28 F4
Mount Pleasant
    (Tenbury Wells) 29 B5
Mount Pleasant Barns 28 F3
Mount Road...................20 F3
Mountbatten Road 22 F6
Mulberry Drive (Gt. Malvern)
    ....23 D5
Mulberry Drive (Upton) ..27 C1
Mulberry Terrace 7 B3
Mulberry Tree Hill 16 G5
Muncaster Place 8 F1
Murren Avenue 24 E3
Myatt Road 18 G4

N

Naboth Court*, Thorneloe Rd.
    ....6 G2
Nailors Row*, Castle Street
    ....20 E2
Nailsworth Close 3 D6
Napleton Lane 14 G4
Narrow Walk (Worcester)..6 F6
Narrow Walk*, Church Lane
    ....12 E3
Nash Close 2 G3
Nash Court*, New St. 30 G4
Nash Court*, Westfield Road
    ....3 C2
Nashs Almshouses*,
    Nashs Passage 30 G4
Nashs Passage..............30 G4
Navigation Road 10 H1
Neason Close 8 F3
Nelson Road 6 F5
Nethergrange Court 21 D6

Nethergrange Flats 21 D6
Netherton Court.............30 E2
Netherton Lane 30 F2
Netherwich Gardens 15 C3
New Bank Street 6 H1
New Chawson Lane 16 F1
New Court 25 B1
New Road (City Centre) 30 E5
New Road (Evesham) 19 B4
New Road (Offenham) ..18 H4
New Road (Pershore) 28 F5
New Street (City Centre)
    ....30 G4
New Street (Evesham) ..20 E3
New Street (Upton) 27 B3
Newark Green..................8 G1
Newbury Road.................6 E3
Newcastle Close 7 D6
Neweys Hill 2 G6
Newland Crescent 5 D6
Newland Drive 16 F4
Newland Lane 16 H6
Newland Road 16 F4/H5
Newlands........................28 F5
Newmans Passage 30 F1
Newport Street 30 E3
Newton Road 21 C4
Newtown Court 21 C5
Newtown Road 7 B4/8 E4
Nibley Close 3 D6
Nightingale Avenue 8 F4
Nightingale Close 16 H6
Nightingale Court*, Cowl St.
    ....20 E2
Nightingale House*,
    Autumn Terrace 7 A4
Nightingale Place 16 H6
Nightingale Road 22 G6
Nine Acres Green 8 E3
Nine Foot Way................16 E4
Ninety Nine Steps 23 C1
Nixon Court (Callow End)
    ....13 D3
Noble View 21 B5
Noele Court*, Tuffrey Cl...6 H1
Nogains........................28 G6
Norbury House*, Friar Street
    ....15 D4
Norfolk Close...................5 D4
Norham Place 8 F1
Norman Close 8 E1
North Bank (Droitwich) ..15 B3
North Croft 6 F6
North End 28 E1
North End Lane ..22 F5/F6/G5
North Hill Court 21 C5
North Hill Gardens.........21 B5
North Malvern Road 21 B5
North Parade 30 E3
North Quay 30 E3

North Road.....

North Road **20** F2
North Street **15** D4
North Walk **23** C1
Northbank, The*,
    Armstrong Drive **6** H6
Northbrook Close **6** H1
Northcliffe House*, Turrall St.
    ....**6** H1
Northcote Street **6** H1
Northern Link Road..**3** A3/4 E4
Northfield Close...............**3** C2
Northfield Lane **13** A3
Northfield Street **30** G1
Northleach Close..............**3** D5
Northwick Avenue **6** G1
Northwick Close **2** F5/G5
Northwick Cottages
    (Rhyse Lane) **29** D3
Northwick Cottages
    (Woofferton Road) ..**29** A4
Northwick Court **2** H6
Northwick House*,
    Boraston Lane **29** B3
Northwick Road (Evesham)
    ....**20** F3
Northwick Road (Worcester)
    ....**2** G2/G5
Northwick Walk................**2** G6
Norton Close **11** A3
Norton Court **12** F6
Norton Road ..**11** A3/B4/C4/D5
Norval Crescent **18** G4
Norwich Road **7** D5
Nuffield Close **6** E3
Nuffield Drive................**16** E1
Nunnery Avenue **16** E3
Nunnery Lane **7** D6
Nunnery Way **8** G4
Nursery Close **28** G4
Nursery Road (Gt. Malvern)
    ....**21** C4
Nursery Road (Worcester)**6** E6
Nursery Walk....................**6** F6
Nurses Houses **29** C6
Nyali House*, Victoria Place
    ....**7** A6

O

O'Keys Lane **3** D2
Oak Apple Close **3** D1
Oak Avenue **7** C1
Oak Close **17** B4
Oak Cottages **11** D4
Oak Crescent **24** G1
Oak Drive **25** B2
Oak Row **27** B3
Oak Street......................**27** B3
Oak Tree Close
    (Tenbury Wells) **29** B3
Oakbridge Court **29** B6

Oakfield Close...............**14** G4
Oakfield Drive **14** G4
Oakfield Road **22** E3
Oakham Drive **16** F2
Oakham Green **16** F2
Oakham Place...............**16** F2
Oakland Avenue **16** F3
Oakland Close...............**27** C1
Oaklands (Gt. Malvern) ..**26** F3
Oaklands (Worcester) **8** E4
Oaklands Court **11** B1
Oaklands, The (Droitwich)
    ....**16** G3
Oaklands, The (Tenbury Wells)
    ....**29** B6
Oakleigh Avenue **1** C3/D3
Oakleigh Heath **1** C3
Oakleigh Road...............**16** F1
Oakmoore Court **15** A1
Oakridge Close **4** E6
Oaks, The **14** G4
Oaktree Close (Evesham)
    ....**20** F4
Oakville Close **10** E2
Oat Street **20** E2
Oatfields **16** G2
Offenham Road..............**20** G2
Offerton Lane **4** F5/H5
Offley Street **6** H1
Ogilvy Square **2** G5
Old Bakery, The*,
    Childswickham Rd...**29** A2
Old Bowling Green Lane
    ....**29** B3
Old Chawson Lane **16** F1
Old Church Road............**25** B1
Old Coach House, The ..**29** C2
Old Coach Road **16** E3
Old Dairy, The*, Swan Lane
    ....**20** E2
Old Drive, The **4** E2
Old Hall Bungalows........**27** D4
Old Hills **13** B4
Old Hollow **21** A6
Old House Farm Cottages
    ....**12** G4
Old Malt House, The **28** G6
Old Malthouse Court*,
    Brewery Walk **6** H2
Old Malvern Road **9** C6
Old Market Court (Droitwich)
    ....**15** D4
Old Market Court (Pershore)
    ....**28** F5
Old Mill Bank, The*, Mill Bank
    ....**20** E2
Old Mill, The **29** A2
Old Music Hall*, High Street
    ....**28** G5
Old Northwick Lane **2** F5

Old Orchard (Gt. Malvern)
    ....**22** E3
Old Orchard (Upton) **27** C1
Old Orchard Lane **25** A1
Old Post Office Lane **17** A5
Old Rectory Close **10** E5
Old Road........................**10** F3
Old Road North **14** G4
Old Road South **14** F5/F6
Old School Close (Offenham)
    ....**18** G3
Old School Close (Pershore)
    ....**28** G5
Old School Court **19** B3
Old School House, The*,
    Merstow Green........**19** D2
Old School Lane **29** B3
Old Street **27** C3
Old Vicarage Close **14** G5
Old Wyche Road **23** B6
Oldbury Road **5** A3/C3/6 E3
Oldwood Road................**29** B6
Ombersley Close............**16** E1
Ombersley Road (Droitwich)
    ....**16** E1
Ombersley Road (Worcester)
    ....**2** G4/H5
Ombersley Street **15** D4
Ombersley Street East ..**15** D4
Ombersley Street West..**15** D3
Ombersley Way.............**16** E1
Ongrils Close..................**28** F4
Ontario Close **10** E3
Orchard Avenue **29** C2
Orchard Close (Hallow)....**1** D4
Orchard Close (Pershore)
    ....**28** F5
Orchard Close (Rushwick)
    ....**9** B1
Orchard Close (Upton) ..**27** B5
Orchard Court **29** B5
Orchard Lea...................**16** F5
Orchard Rise.................**16** G3
Orchard Road (Gt. Malvern)
    ....**23** D2
Orchard Road (Pershore)
    ....**28** F5
Orchard Street................**11** A1
Orchard Walk **19** D4
Orchard Way (Callow End)
    ....**13** D3
Orchard Way*, The Lankets
    ....**17** A5
Orchard, The (Collett's Green)
    ....**9** C6
Orchards, The (Colwall) **25** B2
Orchid Close **11** A4
Orchid Court **24** G3
Orford Way **22** F6
Oriel Close......................**7** B3

Oriel House **21** C6
Orleans Close **19** D5
Orlin Road **25** A1
Orwin Green **8** F3
Osborne Road................**21** D4
Osier Close **11** A2
Osprey Close **10** G3
Ostler Drive **6** E3
Otherton Lane **9** A1
Otley Close **7** D3
Ottawa Close.................**10** E2
Otter Lane **11** C3
Overbrook **20** E4
Overthwart Crescent **8** F2
Owletts End (Evesham)..**20** E3
Owletts End (Pinvin) **28** F1
Oxford Close **7** D5
Oxford Road **21** C5

P

Packers Hill **27** C1
Packhorse Close **6** E4
Packs Close **17** A4
Paddock Close (Droitwich)
    ....**15** C2
Paddock Close (Pershore)
    ....**28** F5
Paddock Green **15** B2
Paddock Hill **15** C2
Paddock Way **15** C2
Paddocks, The **17** D1
Padgewell Hill **16** F2
Padmore Street.............**30** H2
Painswick Close **3** D6
Pakington Road (Droitwich)
    ....**16** E3
Pakington Road (Worcester)
    ....**6** E2
Palmers Green **6** F6
Park Avenue **6** G1
Park Close **22** F4
Park Farm Cottages **24** F5
Park Heath **1** D2
Park Lane (Gt. Malvern) **23** A3
Park Lane (Hallow) **1** D5
Park Lane (Worcester) **6** G1
Park Lane Cottages........**23** A3
Park Road **23** A1
Park Street **30** H4
Park Terrace **29** A5
Park View **23** D2
Park View Terrace **2** G6
Park, The (Gt. Malvern) ..**22** F4
Parker Place **29** B1
Parkfield Cottages **2** E6
Parkfield Lane **1** D6
Parkland Road **2** G4
Parklands (Evesham) **19** C3
Parklands, The
    (Collett's Green) **9** C6

Parklands, The (Droitwich)
...............................16 G4
Parks, The (Evesham)
.......................18 G6/20 G1
Parkside 25 B2
Parsonage Way 8 G2
Parsons Corner 16 F2
Partridge Close 11 A3
Partridge Lane..................5 A1
Passage, The 18 H4
Patterdale Drive 7 D1
Peabody Avenue 8 F3
Peachfield Close 23 D5
Peachfield Road 23 C5
Peachley Gardens...........1 A5
Peachley Lane..................1 A5
Peacock Close 11 C4
Peak View 21 D3
Pear Tree Close 23 C5
Pear Tree Cottages..........1 A3
Pearmain Close................6 E1
Peartree Way 21 A6
Pedlingham Close 25 B2
Peewit Road 19 B3
Pegasus Court................29 A1
Pelham Road 16 G3
Pembroke Avenue...........29 B5
Pembroke Court 29 B4
Pembroke Place 8 G2
Penbury Street 2 H6
Pendas Meadow 28 F2
Pendragon Close 22 G4
Penhill Crescent...........6 E4/E5
Peninsula Road..............11 D5
Penlu Road 29 C3
Penmanor Close 6 E4
Penrice Road 16 G3
Penrith Close...................8 E1
Pentre Villas 15 A6
Pepperpot Mews 27 B3
Perch Road 11 A4
Percheron Way 16 G6
Percy Walton Close........24 E3
Perdiswell Street 2 H6
Perrins Close..................21 C3
Perrins Field 27 C1
Perry Wood Close...........7 C6
Perry Wood Walk 7 B6
Perrycroft Close 3 C2
Perscoran Way 28 F6
Pershore Lane (Hindlip)....4 F1
Pershore Lane (Worcester)
.............................4 H6/8 H1
Pershore Road 19 D4
Pershore Terrace...........28 E2/G1
Peterborough Close 7 C5
Petersfield Drive 16 E6
Peterson Court 23 C1
Petunia Close 11 B4
Pevensey Close 11 B1

Pheasant Street 30 H2
Philip Road 2 H4
Philipscote 20 F2
Phillips Road 29 B1
Phoenix Court 30 G4
Piccadilly*, Main Street ..18 G3
Pickering Green 8 G1
Pickersleigh Avenue 22 E4
Pickersleigh Close.........22 E4
Pickersleigh Grove 22 F5
Pickersleigh Road
.......................22 E4/F5/F6
Pierpoint Court*, Pierpoint St.
.....................................30 F2
Pierpoint Street 30 F2
Piers Close 24 E5
Pike Close 11 A3
Pike Cottages 18 E5
Pilgrim Road 16 E6
Pinder Heights*, Conduit Hill
.....................................20 E2
Pine Close......................3 D2
Pine Way........................7 C1
Pines, The*, Back Lane...29 B2
Pinkett Street 2 G6
Pinkus Close 8 F4
Pippen Field 8 F2
Pirie Avenue 8 F4
Pitchcroft Lane 6 G2
Pitmaston Road 6 F6
Pitmaston Walk 6 F6
Pitt Avenue 8 F4
Pixham Ferry Lane 14 G5
Plantation Drive 8 F2
Players Avenue 22 E3
Plough Croft 8 E2
Ploughmans Close 7 D1
Ploughmans Court 15 C2
Ploughmans Piece 15 B3
Ploughmans Rise 15 B2
Ploughmans Walk*,
     Ploughmans Way 15 B2
Ploughmans Way 15 B2
Plovers Rise 14 G5
Pointon Way..............15 A1/A2
Pole Elm Close 13 D2
Pole Elm Cottages 13 D2
Police Houses (Worcester)
.....................................7 C2
Police Houses*,
     Old Coach Road 16 F3
Police Houses*,
     Stalls Farm Road 16 E3
Pollard Court 10 H1
Pool, The*, Evendene Road
.....................................19 B3
Poolbrook Road.............24 F2
Pope Iron Road...............6 G2
Poplar Avenue..................7 C1
Poplar Close 20 F4

Poplar Court 17 A5
Poplars, The (Badsey)....17 A5
Poplars, The (Wychbold) 15 A5
Port House*, Lowesmoor Ter.
.....................................30 H2
Port Street 20 F3
Portefields Road 7 C3
Porter Road 20 F4
Portland Point*, Armstrong Dr.
.....................................6 H6
Portland Road (Droitwich)
.....................................16 F6
Portland Road (Gt. Malvern)
.....................................23 D1
Portland Street 30 G6
Portland Terrace 6 H6
Portland Walk 6 H6
Portsmouth Close 7 D5
Posey Cottage Court.......1 D3
Post Office Lane
     (Fernhill Heath) 3 D2
Post Office Lane (Kempsey)
.....................................14 G4
Post Office Row..............15 A5
Potters Close...................7 C1
Pound Bank Road 24 F2
Pound Common..............24 F2
Pound Piece Cottages 1 D5
Pound Walk.....................6 G2
Powderham Avenue 8 F1
Powells Row 6 F6
Powick Mills 10 E3
Powick Walk 30 F3
Powyke Court Close 10 E5
Preece Close.................21 D2
Prescott Drive 3 D5
Prestbury Close...............3 D6
Preston Court*, Eastfield Cl.
.....................................3 C2
Prestwich Avenue 7 C6
Price Street 6 H1
Prices Lane 27 B3
Pridzor Close.................15 D6
Pridzor Road 15 D5
Priest Lane 28 G5
Primrose Close 24 G3
Primrose Crescent.........11 A4
Primrose Drive...............11 B4
Primrose House 2 H4
Primsland 16 G3/G4
Primsland Cottages.......16 G6
Primsland Drive 16 F6
Primsland Fields 16 G5
Prince Edwards Close....18 E6
Prince Henrys Close 18 E6
Prince Rupert Avenue ...13 A1
Prince Rupert Road........30 H5
Princes Avenue 16 F4
Princess Margaret Avenue
.....................................22 F3

Princess Road 20 E1
Priors Walk (Evesham) ..20 E3
Priors Walk (Pershore) ..28 F6
Priory Court 23 D2
Priory Gardens 15 D4
Priory Lane 15 D4
Priory Road (Gt. Malvern)
.....................................23 D1/D2
Priory Road (Worcester) 10 F1
Prospect Cottages..........28 E2
Prospect Court 20 G3
Prospect Gardens..........20 G3
Prospect Place 30 H6
Prospect Villas...............15 A5
Providence Street 30 H4
Pryors Green 29 B2
Pulley Lane 16 H3
Pump Street (City Centre)
.....................................30 G4
Pump Street (Gt. Malvern)
.....................................21 C5
Purleigh Avenue 8 F2
Purlieu, The 23 A5
Pye Corner Cottages*,
     Snowshill Road........29 A2
Pyndar Court 22 G2

Q

Quabbs, The 23 A1
Quay House*, Lowesmoor Ter.
.....................................30 H2
Quay Street 30 F4
Quebec Close 10 E2
Queen Elizabeth Almshouses*,
     Upper Tything...........6 H3
Queen Elizabeth Drive ..28 G4
Queen Elizabeth Road ..22 F3
Queen Street (City Centre)
.....................................30 G3
Queen Street (Droitwich)15 D5
Queens Close 21 C4
Queens Drive 23 C1
Queens Mead 27 D3
Queens Road (Evesham)
.....................................19 D1
Queens Road (Gt. Malvern)
.....................................21 C4
Queensgate Mews*, Moor St.
.....................................30 E1
Queenswood Drive 11 B3
Quest Hills Road 21 D4
Quisters 8 F2

R

Race Field 8 F2
Racecourse Road 28 G1
Rack Alley 30 E3
Radnor Croft 3 C6
Raglan Court*, Raglan Street
.....................................6 H1

Raglan Street **6** H1
Rail Ground **28** F5
Railway Terrace (Colwall)
.................................**25** A3
Railway Terrace (Pinvin)**28** E2
Railway Walk **7** A4/B3
Rainbow Court...................**7** B3
Rainbow Hill **7** A3
Rainbow Hill Terrace **7** A3
Rainbow Rise **7** B3
Rainthorpe Avenue **11** B3
Raleigh Close **5** D5
Ramillies Drive **11** C5
Ramsons Close...............**22** G5
Randwick Close **3** D6
Randwick Drive **3** D6
Ranelagh Road **22** F3
Rannoch Avenue **11** C3
Ransom Avenue **11** A2
Raven Drive...................**11** A4
Ravenscroft Drive **16** F6
Ravenshill Close **11** B3
Ravenstone **16** E4
Rea Way **5** D5
Rebekah Gardens.........**16** H4
Rectory Close **1** A6
Rectory Gardens.............**6** G4
Rectory House **27** D4
Rectory Lane................**22** H5
Rectory Place **30** H5
Rectory Road...........**27** C3/D4
Red Lane......................**19** B1
Red Earl Lane...............**24** G2
Red Hill Lane................**11** C1
Redcliffe Street **2** G6
Redfern Avenue **7** C6
Redgate Avenue **29** B5
Redland Close...............**22** E3
Redland Drive **25** B1
Redland House*, Redlands
.................................**28** G5
Redland Road **22** E3
Redlands.......................**28** G4
Redwing Close **21** B2
Redwing House **21** B2
Redwood Close...............**7** C1
Reedham Close **2** G6
Refuge Cottages **29** C5
Regency Mews*,
    Regency Row **22** E3
Regency Road...............**22** E3
Regent House*, School Road
.................................**6** F6
Regiment Close.............**11** C5
Regimental Cottages*,
    Crookbarrow Road ..**11** D5
Regina Close **10** F3
Reindeer Court **30** G3
Reservoir Lane **7** A3
Ribble Close **7** C5

Retreat, The **29** B1
Reynolds Close.............**26** H6
Rhydd Close **24** G3
Rhyse Lane...................**29** C4
Ribston Close **6** E2
Richards Close **21** C2
Richardson Close **15** B5
Richmond Hill **7** A5
Richmond Road (Gt. Malvern)
.................................**22** E3
Richmond Road (Worcester)
.................................**7** A5
Richmonds Pitch **26** E4
Ricketts Lane **15** D4
Ridgeway (Colwall) **25** B6
Ridgeway, The (Droitwich)
.................................**16** E6
Ridgeway, The (Worcester)
.................................**11** C2
Rightons Way **20** E1
Ripley Gardens **8** G1
Ripon Road **7** D4
Ripple Road...................**16** E3
River House*, Common Road
.................................**20** E2
Rivermead Caravan Park
.................................**28** H3
Riverside **29** B4
Riverside Centre **19** D2
Riverside Close **27** B3
Riverside Cottages*, Riverside
.................................**29** B4
Riverside Road **15** D6
Riverside Way **15** D6
Riverview Close **6** E1/F1
Roach Close **11** A4
Robert Owen Court*,
    Wellington Close **30** H4
Robeson Close **16** E6
Robin Close...................**11** A4
Robin Drive **3** B2
Robinia Close **20** E6
Rochford Road **29** B4
Rockingham Lane **8** G1
Rodborough Close **3** D6
Rodborough Drive **3** D6
Rodways Bank **23** B6
Roger Harvey Houses **24** E2
Rogers Hill......................**7** A3
Roland Rutter Court........**28** F5
Roman Way (Droitwich)
.....................**15** C4/**16** E1
Roman Way (Gt. Malvern)
.................................**22** G3
Rona Gardens...............**11** C3
Ronkswood Crescent **7** B4
Ronkswood Hill **7** C4
Rookery Road **14** F3
Rose Avenue (Droitwich)**16** E5
Rose Avenue (Worcester)**7** B3

Rose Bank (Fernhill Heath)
.................................**3** B3
Rose Bank (Worcester)....**7** B6
Rose Hill **7** A6
Rose Terrace...................**7** A5
Rose Villas **15** A5
Rosebank **20** F2
Rosemary Avenue............**5** D5
Rosemary Close **19** B4
Rosemoor Gardens........**11** B3
Rosewood Close **3** C3
Rossendale Close **3** D2
Rothwell Road **26** F2
Rough Meadow **8** E2
Rowan Avenue **7** C3
Rowan Close (Droitwich)
.................................**16** G4
Rowan Close (Evesham)
.................................**20** F4
Rowan Court (Droitwich)
.................................**15** D5
Rowan Court (Worcester) **7** B3
Rowlands Court..............**19** D2
Rowlands House*,
    St. Clements Close ..**6** G5
Rowley Hill Street **6** F5
Rowntree Gardens **8** F4
Royal Albert Close **30** H6
Royal Court **30** H6
Royal Oak Gardens **22** F3
Royal Well Court **23** B5
Rudd Close **11** A4
Rudge Road **19** D1
Rushers Close **28** F4
Rushy Close **16** F3
Russell Close (Collett's Green)
.................................**9** C6
Russell Close (Gt. Malvern)
.................................**22** E4
Russell Cottages **29** B2
Russell Court.................**29** A2
Russell Drive **22** E4
Russell House*,
    St. Clements Close ..**6** G5
Russell Square **29** B2
Russell Terrace **29** A2
Russet Close **6** E1
Rutland Place **11** C3
Ryall Court Lane **27** A5
Ryall Grove*, The Grove
.................................**27** B6
Ryall Lane.....................**27** B5
Ryall Meadow **27** B5
Rydal Close **7** D2
Rye Close **16** E5
Rye Lea, The **16** F2
Rye Place **8** G1
Ryeland Close.................**3** C6
Rynal Place **20** E2
Rynal Street..................**20** E2

S

Sabrina Avenue **2** G6/**6** G1
Sabrina Terrace **6** G2
Sabrina Walk...................**2** G6
Saddlers Walk **7** C1
Saddlestones..................**29** A1
Salamanca Drive...........**11** C5
Salisbury Close **7** D5
Salisbury Cottages*,
    Defford Road **28** G6
Salisbury Drive **19** D4
Salt Box Lane*, Oldwood Rd.
.................................**29** B6
Salt Way **15** D4
Salters Close...................**7** C1
Salters Court*, Galton Way
.................................**16** E6
Salters Shopping Centre **15** D4
Saltwood Avenue............**8** F4
Salubrious **29** C2
Salwarpe Close **15** A5
Salwarpe Road **15** D3
Sanctuary Close **6** E5
Sandles Close **16** H4
Sandles Road **16** H4
Sandown Road **19** D4
Sandpiper Close **1** B3
Sandpiper Crescent.......**21** B2
Sandringham Close
    (Evesham) **20** E1
Sandringham Close
    (Gt. Malvern) **22** G2
Sands Close **29** B1
Sands Lane **17** B6
Sands, The **29** B1
Sandscroft Avenue **29** C1
Sandys Road (Gt. Malvern)
.................................**22** G4
Sandys Road (Worcester)
.................................**6** G1
Sansome Fields House..**30** G1
Sansome Fields Walk **30** F1
Sansome Mews*,
    St. Oswalds Road....**30** F1
Sansome Place.............**30** G2
Sansome Street............**30** G2
Sansome Walk **30** F1
Santler Court*, Worcester Rd.
.................................**22** E4
Sapphire Crescent...........**6** E4
Sarai Close **16** H4
Saunders Street **2** G6
Sawmill Close **7** B5
Saxonbury **20** E4
Sayers Avenue **21** C3
Scafell Close **7** D2
Scholars Walk **16** F3
School Bank **3** A2
School Close **28** F1

School Cottages 1 D3
School Lane (Badsey) 17 A6
School Lane (Upton) 27 B3
School Road (Evesham) 19 B3
School Road (Worcester)..6 F6
School Road (Wychbold)15 A6
School Walk 12 E3
Scobell Close.................28 F4
Scotland Place 29 B4
Scotlands, The 15 B2
Sebright Avenue 7 B6
Sebright Close 28 F4
Sedge Close 5 D5
Selborne Road 6 G2
Selborne Road West........6 G2
Selsey Close 4 E6
Seven Acres 8 E3
Severn Cottages 27 B2
Severn Court 16 E5
Severn Drive (Gt. Malvern)
..............................24 G2
Severn Drive (Upton)......27 B3
Severn Grange 2 F3
Severn House*,
    St. Clements Close ..6 G5
Severn Street.................30 F6
Severn Terrace 30 E1
Severn Way
..........10 H2/H6/14 E5/F1
Severndale 16 F2
Seward Close 20 E2
Seward Road.................17 A5
Seymour Avenue 2 G5
Seymour Court 22 E2
Shaftesbury Green 8 F4
Shakespeare Road 5 D4
Shambles, The 30 G3
Shannon Way 20 G3
Shap Drive.......................8 E1
Sharman Close 6 G2
Sharman Road 6 G2
Sharpe Road.................10 G1
Shaw Mews 30 F2
Shaw Street...................30 F2
Shaw Walk....................22 F5
Shawcross Walk 20 E3
Shear House 29 C2
Sheepscombe Drive 3 D6
Sheffield Close 7 D6
Sheldon Avenue 29 C1
Sheldon Close (Pershore)
..............................28 F4
Sheldon Close (Wychbold)
..............................15 B5
Sheldon Park Road.........2 G3
Shelley Close 3 A6
Shelsley Drive 23 B6
Shenstone Close...........24 G1
Shepherds Close...........15 C3
Shepherds Court............15 C2

Shepherds Green 15 C3
Shepherds Hill...............15 C3
Shepherds Place...........15 C3
Shepherds Pool.............19 D1
Shepherds Rise.............15 C2
Shepherds Way.............15 C2
Sheridan Row 8 F3
Sheringham Road 11 B3
Sherrands Green Road ..24 F1
Sherwood Green 24 F1
Sherriff Street 7 B4
Sherwood Lane 10 F2
Shetland Close 3 B6
Shipston Close 3 D5
Shipwrights Close 7 C1
Shire Way 16 G6
Shirley Close 22 F6
Shirley Jones Close 15 D2
Shirley Road 16 G3
Shopping Centre, The ...20 F4
Shor Street 20 E3
Shoulton Lane 1 B3
Showell Close 16 H3
Showell Green...............16 H3
Showell Grove...............16 H4
Showell Road 16 H3
Shrawley Road 3 C2
Shrub Hill........................7 B4
Shrub Hill Road 7 A4
Shrubbery Avenue 6 H2
Shrubbery Road 6 H2
Shuttlefast Lane 26 G2
Sidbury 30 G5
Sidbury House 30 G5
Silver Street (City Centre)
..............................30 G3
Silver Street (Colwall) 25 B2
Silverdale Avenue 7 C6
Simon de Montfort Drive18 E5
Simons Way 20 E4
Sinclair Court*, Bewdley St.
..............................19 D2
Singer Hill 16 F2
Sinton Terrace 6 F6
Six Acres Croft 8 E3
Skenfrith Place 8 F1
Skiddaw Close.................8 E1
Skinner Road...................6 F6
Skinner Street 6 F6
Skipton Crescent 4 F6
Sky Court*, Checketts Lane
..............................2 H5
Skyrrold Road 24 G1
Slade Avenue 8 E2
Slimbridge Close 11 B3
Sling Lane (Gt. Malvern) 21 D6
Sling Lane (Hindlip)..........4 E2
Sling Pool Walk 30 E5
Smallbrook Road*,
    Leamington Road 29 B1
Smite Caravan Park 4 G3

Smite Lane 4 G2/H3
Smith Court 30 H6
Smiths Avenue 6 E6
Smiths Way 28 F6
Snowberry Avenue 8 E3
Snowshill Close 4 E6
Snowshill Road 29 A2
Snowshill View*, Snowshill Rd.
..............................29 A2
Solent Place 20 F3
Solent Road 7 C4
Solitaire Avenue 6 E4
Somers Court 21 D3
Somers Park Avenue 21 C4
Somers Road (Gt. Malvern)
..............................21 D4
Somers Road (Worcester)
..............................6 G2
Somerset Place...............6 H2
Somerville Road 7 B4
Sorrel Close....................3 B2
Sorrel Way 24 G3
South Croft 6 F6
South Lawns 23 C5
South Parade................30 F4
South Park Drive 15 C2
South Quay 30 F4
South Street 30 H4
Southall Avenue 2 G5
Southdown Road.............3 C6
Southfield Street 30 G1
Southwold Close 11 B3
Spa Road 16 E4
Sparrowhall Lane 9 B6
Sparrowhawk Close........22 F4
Spellis Green Cottages 3 D4
Spencer Drive 24 E2
Spencers Walk 22 F3
Spenser Road 5 D4
Spetchley Road 11 D1
Spindle Road 22 G5
Spinney Grove................20 F5
Spinney, The 6 E2
Spion Kop 28 E2
Spring Bank (Hindlip) 3 C5
Spring Close (Colwall) 25 B1
Spring Close (Tenbury Wells)
..............................29 B3
Spring Court 22 G4
Spring Gardens (City Centre)
..............................30 H3
Spring Gardens (Gt. Malvern)
..............................22 F3
Spring Gardens
    (Tenbury Wells) 29 C4
Spring Grove Lane*,
    Oldwood Road 29 B6
Spring Hill 7 A4
Spring Lane (Gt. Malvern)
..............................22 F4

Spring Lane (Worcester) ..7 A5
Spring Lane South...........22 F4
Spring Meadow 8 E3
Springbank (Gt. Malvern)
..............................21 D6
Springfield Close 11 B3
Springfield Drive 20 E5
Springfield Glade............21 D3
Springfield Lane 29 A1
Springfield Road 11 B2
Squires Close 14 F4
Squires Walk 14 F4
Squires, The 17 C4
Squirrel Drive 11 C3
St. Agathas Close 28 G5
St. Agathas Road 28 G5
St. Agathas Court*, Head St.
..............................28 F5
St. Albans Close 7 D4
St. Andrew Road 19 B4
St. Andrews Close.........16 E4
St. Andrews Court 16 E4
St. Andrews Drive 16 E4
St. Andrews Gardens 30 F4
St. Andrews Road (Droitwich)
..............................16 E4
St. Andrews Road
    (Gt. Malvern) 23 D5
St. Andrews Road (Pershore)
..............................28 F6
St. Andrews Square 15 D4
St. Andrews Street 15 D4
St. Annes Close 2 H4
St. Annes Road (Worcester)
..............................2 H4
St. Anns Road (Gt. Malvern)
..............................23 C1
St. Audries Road 11 A1
St. Augustine Close.......15 C5
St. Augustine Drive 15 D5
St. Barnabas Hostel 22 G2
St. Bernard Drive............24 E4
St. Catherines Hill 7 B6
St. Catherines Road 20 E5
St. Catherines Vale 7 B6
St. Christopher Court 17 D6
St. Davids Drive 19 D5
St. Clements Close 6 G5
St. Clements Court 6 G5
St. Clements Gardens......6 G5
St. Clouds Cottages 13 C5
St. Dunstans Close 11 A1
St. Dunstans Crescent 7 A6
St. Egwine Close.............6 H2
St. Egwins Road (Evesham)
..............................20 E1
St. Egwins Road (Norton)
..............................18 E1
St. Georges Close 20 E6
St. Georges Crescent 15 D5

St. Georges Lane North ..6 H2
St. Georges Lane South ..6 H2
St. Georges Square
(Droitwich) 15 D5
St. Georges Square
(Worcester) 6 H2
St. Georges Walk 6 H2
St. James Close 17 A5
St. James Crescent 21 A5
St. James Drive (Evesham)
..................................20 E5
St. James Drive (Gt. Malvern)
..................................21 D6
St. James Road..............21 D6
St. Johns 6 F6
St. Johns Close (Evesham)
..................................20 E6
St. Johns Close (Worcester)
....................................2 H4
St. Johns Home 16 E5
St. Johns Mews*, St. Johns
....................................6 F6
St. Josephs Close 16 E2
St. Kitts Close 21 D3
St. Lawrence Close 10 F2
St. Lawrence Road 19 D2
St. Lukes Close 20 E6
St. Margarets Road 19 D5
St. Marks Close (Evesham)
..................................20 E5
St. Marks Close (Worcester)
..................................11 A2
St. Martins Gate 30 H3
St. Martins House 30 H3
St. Marys Close (Kempsey)
..................................14 F4
St. Marys Close
(Tenbury Wells) 29 B4
St. Marys Court 30 G1
St. Marys Road (Droitwich)
..................................16 F4
St. Marys Road (Evesham)
..................................20 E1
St. Marys Street............30 F1
St. Matthews Close 20 E5
St. Michaels Close..........20 E6
St. Michaels Court*,
Gresham Road 5 D4
St. Michaels Road 2 H5
St. Milburgh Close..........18 G4
St. Moritz Close 2 F5
St. Nicholas House 21 B5
St. Nicholas Lane 4 G6
St. Nicholas Street
(City Centre)............30 G3
St. Nicholas Street (Droitwich)
..................................16 E3
St. Oswalds Almshouses*,
St. Oswalds Road....30 F1
St. Oswalds Close............6 H3

St. Oswalds Road 30 F1
St. Patricks Close 19 D6
St. Pauls Close 20 E6
St. Pauls Court*, St. Pauls St.
..................................30 H4
St. Pauls Street 30 H4
St. Pauls Walk*, St. Pauls St.
..................................30 H3
St. Peters Church Lane ..16 F5
St. Peters Close (Evesham)
..................................20 F3
St. Peters Close (Gt. Malvern)
..................................26 F4
St. Peters Court 16 F4
St. Peters Crescent 16 E5
St. Peters Drive 11 A4
St. Peters Gardens 16 E5
St. Peters Hill..................11 A4
St. Peters Road (Droitwich)
..................................16 F4
St. Peters Road (Gt. Malvern)
..................................21 B4
St. Peters Street 30 G5
St. Peters Walk 16 E5
St. Philips Drive 19 D6
St. Richards Close..........15 A6
St. Richards Gardens 16 E3
St. Richards Road (Evesham)
..................................19 D5
St. Richards Road (Wychbold)
..................................15 A6
St. Saviours Court 22 F3
St. Stephens Street..........6 H1
St. Stephens Terrace 6 H1
St. Swithins Close 7 B6
St. Swithins Street..........30 G3
St. Wulstans Close 20 E6
St. Wulstans Crescent......7 A5
St. Wulstans Drive 26 F4
St. Wulstons Court 30 G1
Stafford Avenue 8 G1
Stainburn Avenue 5 D5
Stainburn Close...............5 D5
Stallard Road....................6 E2
Stalls Farm Estate*,
Stalls Farm Road 16 E3
Stalls Farm Road............16 E3
Stanage Close..................8 E2
Stanbrook House Road...13 D3
Stanbrook Road 29 B3
Stanhope Court*, Malvern Rd.
..................................10 F1
Stanier Road 4 F6
Stanley Road (Gt. Malvern)
..................................24 E1
Stanley Road (Worcester)
....................................7 A5
Stanley Street 11 A2
Stanmore Road 10 F2
Stanway Close 3 C6

Staplow Road 8 E6
Star Cottages 29 B4
Star Lane...........................6 F6
Starling Close 11 A4
Station Bungalows..........25 B2
Station Cottages*, Station Rd.
..................................29 A1
Station Drive 25 B2
Station Road (Broadway)
..................................29 A1
Station Road (Fernhill Heath)
....................................3 D3
Station Road (Offenham)18 H5
Station Road (Pershore)
..................28 G2/G3/G4
Station Street 15 D3
Station Walk 7 B4
Steamer Point 22 F6
Stella Villas*, Star Lane....6 F6
Stephen Close...............25 A5
Stephenson Road 6 G2
Stephenson Terrace 6 G3
Steynors Avenue 16 E3
Steynors Close 16 E3
Stirling Avenue 4 F6
Stock Coppice Close........8 E1
Stoke Road 15 B5
Stokesay Lane 4 G6
Stone Close...................25 B2
Stone Court 25 B2
Stone Drive 25 B1
Stone Wall Cottages 1 D1
Stoneleigh Close 11 B4
Stonewall Terrace 28 F6
Stoney Croft Close 3 C3
Stoneycroft Close...........3 C3
Stony Close 8 E2
Storer Court 24 F2
Stotfield Avenue 8 F2
Stouton Croft 15 D3
Stowe Lane 25 A3
Strand Lane......................4 E1
Stroma Avenue 11 C3
Stuart Rise 11 C1
Sudeley Avenue 8 F1
Sudeley Close 21 D2
Sudgrove Close...............3 C5
Suffolk Drive 3 C5
Suffolk Way 16 F6
Summer Street 6 H1
Summerfield Gardens 19 B4
Summerfield Road..........22 E3
Sundew Close 3 B2
Sunnyside 28 G5
Sunnyside Caravan Park..3 A4
Sunnyside Close 14 F4
Sunnyside Road 6 H1
Sunrise 22 E6
Surman Street 30 F1
Swaledale Court 8 E1

Swallow Close 11 B3
Swallow Place 16 H6
Swallowfield....................8 F3
Swan Close 29 B3
Swan Court (Evesham) ..20 F3
Swan Court (Tenbury Wells)
..................................29 B3
Swan Drive 15 D6
Swan Lane (Evesham) ..20 E2
Swan Lane (Tenbury Wells)
..................................29 C3
Swanpool Walk 6 F6
Swans Reach*, Swan Lane
..................................20 E2
Swinesherd Way 12 E1
Swinton Close 6 E6
Swinton Lane 6 E6/F2
Sycamore Avenue 20 F4
Sycamore Close 21 D2
Sycamore Road................7 B2
Sydney Street 6 H1
Synehurst 17 A5
Synehurst Avenue 17 A5
Synehurst Crescent........17 A5

T

Tabor Gardens 22 E5
Tagwell Close 16 G6
Tagwell Gardens 16 F5
Tagwell Road..................16 F4
Talavera Road................11 D5
Tallow Hill 7 A4
Tamar Close 7 B4
Tamar Place 20 F3
Tamarisk Close 3 B2
Tamworth Avenue 8 F1
Tan House Cottages 9 C2
Tan House Lane 9 C2
Tanglewood Heights 21 B4
Tanhouse Lane 21 C2/D2
Tanners Close..................7 C1
Tannery Court 29 B5
Tannery Mews*, Carden St.
..................................30 H4
Tansy Close 11 A4
Tantallon Close 8 F1
Tappenhall Road..............3 C3
Tarrys Row 20 E2
Tattersall 8 F3
Tavern Orchard 8 F2
Tay Avenue....................11 C3
Taylors Court*, Taylors Lane
..................................30 F2
Taylors Lane (Cherry Acre)
..................................11 A5
Taylors Lane (City Centre)
..................................30 F2
Tayson Way 21 D2
Tearne Street 6 E3
Teasel Close 11 A4

Teasel Way 3 B3
Teesdale Close 16 F2
Teeswater Close 3 B6
Teme Avenue 24 G2
Teme Court (Tenbury Wells)
.........................29 B4
Teme Court (Worcester) 10 E3
Teme Crescent 16 G2
Teme House*, Henwick Road
.........................6 F3
Teme Road 7 C3
Teme Street..................29 B4
Temeside Close 29 C4
Temeside Way...............10 F4
Temeside*, Malvern Road
..............................10 F3
Temperence Street 30 H4
Temple Mews 19 D2
Ten Acres 15 B3
Tench Close 11 A4
Tennis Walk 6 H3
Tennyson Close 3 A6
Tennyson Drive 21 D6
Terrace Road...........28 E2/G1
Terrace Walk 7 A3
Terrill Court 19 D2
Terrills Lane..................29 B6
Tetbury Drive...................7 D1
Tewkesbury Road 27 B6
Thackholme 8 F2
Thames Close 7 B5
Thames Drive 16 F2
Thatchers Close 15 B3
Thatchers Court..............15 B2
Thatchers Green 15 B2
Thatchers Piece 15 B2
Thatchers Place 15 B2
Thatchers Way 15 B2
Thetford Avenue 8 G1
Thirlmere Close 8 E1
Thirlstane Road..............23 D3
Thistle Close (Fernhill Heath)
..............................3 B2
Thistle Close (Worcester)
..............................11 B4
Thistledown 19 D6
Thomas Close 3 B3
Thomas Morris House*,
Laburnum Walk 27 C3
Thorn Avenue 7 C1
Thorn Lea 20 G4
Thorneloe Court*,
Barbourne Crescent..6 G2
Thorneloe Road 6 G2
Thorneloe Walk 6 H2
Thorngrove Mews 1 C1
Thorngrove Road 24 E2
Three Cocks Lane..........18 H4
Three Springs Road 28 E6
Threshfield Drive 8 E3

Thrift Villas 1 D3
Tibberton Mews..............23 D2
Tibberton Road 23 D1
Till Street 7 A2
Timberdine Avenue 11 A1
Timberdine Close 11 A1
Tintern Avenue 7 B1
Tiree Avenue 11 C3
Tiverton Close 4 F6
Toftdale Green 8 E3
Toll House Close.............9 C1
Tolladine Road 7 A4
Tolladine Terrace*,
Tolladine Road 8 E1
Tollhouse Drive 6 F4
Topham Avenue 8 F4
Toronto Close 10 E3
Torridon Walk 11 C3
Toulouse Drive 11 D5
Tower Hill 15 D5
Tower Road 6 G1
Town Acres 8 E2
Towneley........................8 G4
Townsend Street.............6 G2
Treacle Nook 8 E2
Treadwells Row*,
Littleworth Street 19 D2
Tredennyke*, Barbour Terrace
..............................6 G2
Trefoil Close (Gt. Malvern)
..............................24 G3
Trefoil Close (Worcester)11 B4
Trehearn Road 15 D6
Trelawney Close 6 F6
Trench Lane 16 H6
Trent Close 16 G2
Trent Road 7 C4
Trevithick Close 8 F3
Trimnel Green 16 F3
Trinity Close 20 E4
Trinity Passage*, Angel Lane
..............................30 F3
Trinity Road....................21 C5
Trinity Street 30 G3
Trinity, The*, Trinity Street
..............................30 G3
Trotshill Lane East...........8 F2
Trotshill Lane West 8 E2
Trotshill Way 8 G3
Troutbeck Drive................7 D2
Trow Way 10 H2
Truro Gardens.................7 D5
Tudor Close 24 F4
Tudor Way......................5 D4
Tuffrey Close 6 H1
Tunnel Hill (Upton) 27 C2
Tunnel Hill (Worcester) 7 B2
Turbary Avenue 8 F2
Turners Close 7 C1
Turnpike Close 6 F4

Turrall Street 6 H1
Tutbury Row 8 G1
Twarnley Rise 8 F4
Tweed Close 7 C5
Twinberrow Court 21 D3
Tyddesley Wood Lane....28 E6
Tyndale 8 F3
Tyne Close 7 C5
Tyne Drive.....................20 G3
Tyning, The 16 F2
Tythbridge Street 6 G5
Tythe Barn Cottages 17 D2
Tythe Road 29 B1
Tything Court*, The Tything
..............................6 H3
Tything, The 6 H3

U

Ullswater Close 7 D2
Ulverston Green 7 D1
Unicorn Walk 30 F3
Union Lane 15 D3
Union Place.....................2 G6
Union Street 30 G4
Upper Battenhall 11 C2
Upper Chase Road 24 F2
Upper Court....................25 B1
Upper Ferry Lane 13 C3
Upper Ground 8 E1
Upper Hook Road 27 B2
Upper Howsell Road 21 D3
Upper Interfields 21 C1
Upper Park Street 7 A6
Upper Tything 6 H3
Upper Welland Road 26 E4
Upper Wick Lane.............9 C1
Upton Gardens 27 C4
Upton Road (Callow End)
..........................13 C1/C4
Upton Road (Powick) 10 E5
Upton Snodsbury Road ..28 F1

V

Vale House*, Common Road
..............................20 E2
Vale Link 20 F6
Vale Park*, Crab Apple Way
..............................20 F6
Valentine Close.............16 G6
Valley Walk 16 E2
Valley Way 16 E2
Vancouver Close 10 E2
Vandra Close.................22 F2
Vauxhall Street 7 B2
Vernon Grove 15 D3
Vernon Park Road 6 F6
Vesta Tilley Court 30 H3
Vetch Field Avenue 8 E3
Vicar Street 7 B2
Vicarage Close 1 D4

Vicarage Court*, St. Pauls St.
..............................30 H4
Vicarage Lane 3 A1
Victoria Avenue (Droitwich)
..............................16 F4
Victoria Avenue (Evesham)
..............................20 E1
Victoria Avenue (Worcester)
..............................7 B5
Victoria Institute*,
Sansome Walk 30 F1
Victoria Lane 6 G1
Victoria Park Road 22 E4
Victoria Place 7 A6
Victoria Road..................21 D6
Victoria Square 15 D4
Victoria Street 6 G1
Victoria Terrace 28 F5
Victoria Walk*, North Hill Gdns.
..............................21 C5
Victoria Walk (Gt. Malvern)
..............................23 D1
Viewfields 8 E4
Vigornia Avenue 7 A2
Vigornia Cottages*,
Droitwich Road..........3 D2
Vimiera Close 11 D5
Vincent Road...................7 A5
Vine Court*, Vine St. 19 D2
Vine Mews.....................19 D2
Vine Street (Evesham) ..19 D2
Vine Street (Worcester) ..2 G6
Vinery Mews 29 B4
Vines Lane................15 C4/D4
Vines Mews...................15 D4
Vintners Close.................7 C1
Viscount Cobham Court 22 F6
Vivian Avenue 9 C1

W

Wadborough Road 12 F6
Wadley Drive...................2 G3
Waggon Place 8 E2
Wain Green 8 E2
Wainwright Road 4 E5/F6
Wakefield Close 7 D5
Wakeman Street 6 H1
Walcot Lane 28 G1
Walkers Lane 12 E2
Walkmill Drive 15 A4
Walkworth Avenue...........4 F6
Wallcroft Close 6 E3
Walmer Crescent............4 F6
Walnut Avenue 7 C1
Walnut Close 29 B2
Walnut Court 7 C1
Walnut Crescent 23 D5
Walsgrove Court 30 F2
Walton Court 26 F2
Walton Mews 26 F2

Walwyn Road 25 A4
Warden Green...................7 D2
Wardour Place..................8 F1
Wards Close 20 G3
Warehouse Court 30 G1
Warmstry Court*, Quay Street
.................................30 F4
Warndon Lane 8 G1
Warndon Way 4 H6
Warwick Court*, Abbey Road
.................................23 C2
Warwick House*, Wells Road
.................................23 C2
Wasdale Court.................8 E1
Waseley Close 11 C3
Washbrook Close 4 E6
Washington Street 30 G1
Wassage Court 15 A2
Wassage Way 15 A2
Wassage Way North 15 A2
Wassage Way South 15 A2
Watchetts Green 8 F2
Water Croft 8 E2
Waterford Close 2 G6
Waterloo Close 22 H3
Waterloo House 30 G1
Waters Edge 6 H6
Waters Reach 6 H6
Waterside (Droitwich)
.................................15 D5/D6
Waterside (Evesham) ...19 D4
Waterside (Upton) 27 B3
Waterside Close 15 D5
Waterside Park 4 F5
Waterworks Road 6 G1
Waterworks Walk 6 G1
Watery Lane (Gt. Malvern)
.................................26 F5
Watery Lane (Worcester)..6 E6
Watkins Way 24 G3
Waveney Road 16 F2
Waverley Street.............11 A1
Wayside Cottages*,
Worcester Road 29 B3
Weaver Close 15 D5
Weavers Court 2 H5
Webb Drive 15 B5
Wedderburn Road..........24 G1
Wedgberrow Close 16 E4
Wedley Place..................8 F4
Weighing Machine Cottages*,
Boraston Lane 29 B3
Weir Gardens 28 G6
Weir House*, Cowl Street
.................................20 E2
Weir Lane 10 G2
Weir Meadows Holiday Park
.................................20 F2
Welland Close................16 G2
Welland Road 27 C1

Wellesley Court*,
Bransford Road 6 F6
Wellington Close 30 H4
Wellingtonia, The...........23 B5
Wells Close 26 E4
Wells Gardens...............29 C1
Wells Road (Gt. Malvern)
.........................23 C1/C6
Wells Road (Worcester) ..7 D4
Wensleydale 16 F2
Wensleydale Drive 3 C6
Wentworth Court 6 H1
Werstan Close 24 F3
West Bank......................15 C3
West End*, Snowshill Road
.................................29 A2
West Malvern Road ..21 A6/B5
West Park Drive 15 D2
West Stone 15 B3
West Street 19 D2
West View*, Swan La...20 E2
Westbourne Close 6 F4
Westbury Avenue 16 F2
Westbury Court 16 F1
Westbury Lodge 30 H1
Westbury Street 30 H1
Westcroft Court*, Westcroft St.
.................................15 D4
Westcroft Street 15 D4
Westfield Close 3 C2
Westfield Road 3 C2
Westhaven Place............6 F2
Westlands Walk 15 C2
Westlands Way 16 E2
Westlea Close 5 D6
Westlyn Close 22 E4
Westmead Close............15 D3
Westmead House 15 D3
Westminster Bank 23 A1
Westminster Road
(Gt. Malvern) 23 C5
Westminster Road (Worcester)
.................................7 D5
Westmount Close 10 F2
Weston Villas*, London Road
.................................30 H6
Westonbirt Close...........11 C3
Westview 20 E2
Westview Close...............5 D5
Westview Terrace 29 B4
Westward Road.............21 C2
Westwood Avenue.........16 F4
Westwood Close 16 E1
Westwood Road 15 D2
Westwood Way 16 E1
Wey Close 16 E2
Wey Place 16 E2
Weyburn Close 10 F2
Wharf House*,
Lowesmoor Ter. 30 H2

Wharfedale Crescent 16 G2
Wharfedale Drive............8 E3
Wheatfield Avenue 11 A3
Wheatfield Cottages 3 D1
Wheatfield Court 13 C1
Wheatfields Park 13 D2
Wheeler Close 6 F4
Wheeler Orchard 29 B6
Wheelwright Close 7 C1
Whinfield Gardens 2 G4
Whinfield Road 2 G4
Whitakers Close 28 F4
Whitborn Close 24 G2
Whitborn End 24 G2
Whitcroft Road 28 G4
White Castle 8 G1
White Hill 8 E3
White Horse Close 10 E3
White Ladies Close 6 H2
White Ladies Walk 6 H3
Whitehall Close 9 C1
Whites Court 10 G1
Whites Road 10 F2
Whitethorn Grove 22 G5
Whitewood Close 10 E1
Whitewood Way 11 D1
Whitmore Road 5 D6
Whittingham Court*, Tower Hill
.................................15 D5
Whittingham House.......15 D5
Whittington Gate 11 D1
Whittington Road...........11 D1
Wickhamford Lane 20 H4
Wigton Place 7 D1
Wilberforce Place 8 F4
Wildwood Drive 8 F6
Wilfred Close 7 A2
Willersey Road 17 A6
Willets Road 16 G4
William Crescent 19 D2
William House*,
St. Christopher Ct. ..17 D6
William Shakespeare Place
.................................16 G4
William Tennant Way 27 C4
Williams Court*, Battisto Walk
.................................24 F1
Williamson Road 7 B5
Willmott House*, Rynal Place
.................................20 E2
Willow Close (Fernhill Heath)
.................................3 D2
Willow Close (Pershore) 28 E4
Willow Close (Pinvin)......28 F1
Willow Close (Upton).....27 B6
Willow Court (Droitwich) 15 D2
Willow Court*, Autumn Ter.
.................................7 A4
Willow Drive 16 G4
Willow Grove 22 E5

Willow Road 20 G4
Willow Street 30 G6
Willows, The*, Back La...29 A2
Willowslea Road 2 G4
Wilmot Road 21 D3
Wilson Street 7 B3
Wilton Road 24 F1
Winchcombe Drive 3 C6
Winchester Avenue 6 F6
Windermere Drive....3 C6/7 D1
Windles Row 8 F2
Windmeres 20 F2
Windmill Close 6 G2
Windmill Cottages 3 C1
Windmill Lane 14 G2
Windrush Close 7 C5
Windrush Crescent 24 H2
Windrush House*,
Henwick Road 6 F3
Windsor Avenue 6 E5
Windsor Close 22 G2
Windsor Road 16 G4
Windsor Row 30 G3
Wingfield Avenue............4 F6
Winnetts Lane 15 D4
Winnipeg Close 10 E2
Winslow Avenue 16 E6
Winsmore 10 E6
Winterburn Road 2 E6
Wirlpiece Avenue 8 G2
Wise Lack Place 8 E3
Withers Road 6 G6
Withincroft 8 F3
Witney Court 3 D6
Witton Avenue 16 F2
Wolsey Close 7 C4
Wolverton Road...............7 A3
Wood End 20 E5
Wood Farm Road 26 F2
Wood Leason Avenue 8 F2
Wood Piece Close...........4 E6
Wood Terrace (City Centre)
.................................30 G1
Wood Terrace (Pershore)
.................................28 F6
Woodbine Road 6 G2
Woodbridge Close.........11 B2
Woodbury Lane 12 F6
Woodbury Park 12 G6
Woodbury Rise 21 C4
Woodfield Cottages.......15 D6
Woodfield Road.............15 D5
Woodfields 15 D5
Woodgreen Drive ..8 E2/E3/F1
Woodhouse Close 10 H1
Woodland Close 3 B6
Woodland Cottages*,
Little Chestnut St. 7 A3
Woodland Piece 20 F5
Woodland Road..............7 B1

Woodlands (Evesham) ..**20** E5
Woodlands (Kempsey) ..**14** G4
Woodlands Close **26** E3
Woodlands, The (Upton)
...............................**27** B5
Woodmancote **3** D6
Woodmans Close **15** C2
Woodmans Green **15** C2
Woodmans Place **15** C2
Woodmans Rise **15** C2
Woodmans Way **15** C2
Woodrow House*,
The Holloway **15** D5
Woodrow Houses **15** D5
Woodshears Alley **23** D2
Woodshears Drive..........**23** D2
Woodshears Road **23** D2
Woodside Cottages..........**4** E4
Woodside Road...............**7** C6
Woodstock Road..............**6** E4
Woodward Close **28** F6
Woodward Road **28** F6
Woodyatt Court **24** E2
Woofferton Road **29** A4
Woolhope Rise*,
Woolhope Road **7** A6
Woolhope Road...............**7** A6
Woolmead Row...............**8** G2
Worboys Road................**10** F1
Worcester Road (Droitwich)
...................**16** E4/G3/H2
Worcester Road (Evesham)
.....................**17** C4/**19** D1
Worcester Road (Gt. Malvern)
...............................**22** G2
Worcester Road (Kempsey)
...............................**14** G2
Worcester Road (Pershore)
...............................**28** E4
Worcester Road
(Tenbury Wells) **29** B3
Worcester Road (Worcester)
...............................**11** A5
Worcester Road (Wychbold)
...............................**15** A5
Worcestershire, The **16** E4
Wordsworth Avenue **7** A1
Wordsworth Green **21** D5
Workman Road **19** B3
Worthington Gardens **8** F3
Wren Avenue **22** G6
Wren Close **3** B2
Wryflatt **8** F2
Wulfstan House*, Henwick Rd.
...................................**6** F3
Wyatt Court*, New St. **30** G4
Wyatt Mews*, Union Street
...............................**30** G4
Wych Elm Close **7** C6
Wych Road (Droitwich) ..**16** F3

Wychbold Court*,
Worcester Road **15** A6
Wyche Road (Gt. Malvern)
...............................**23** B5
Wye Avenue **24** G2
Wye Close (Droitwich) ..**16** G3
Wye Close (Worcester) **7** B4
Wykewane **24** G2
Wylds Lane **7** B4/**30** H5
Wyre Road **28** G2

Y

Yarrow Close..................**11** A4
Yates Court*, High St. **19** D2
Yates Hay Road **21** C3
Yew Tree Close (Colwall)
...............................**25** A5
Yew Tree Close (Evesham)
...............................**20** G5
Yew Tree Close (Worcester)
...............................**11** C1
Yew Tree Court (Broadway)
...............................**29** C2
Yew Tree Court (Worcester)
...............................**11** C4
Yew Tree Hill..................**16** G4
Yew Tree Lane
(Fernhill Heath) **3** D2
Yew Tree Lane (Gt. Malvern)
...............................**26** F4
Yewleigh Lane................**27** D1
York Avenue **16** F4
York Close **22** F2
York Place......................**6** G3
York Place Lane **6** G3

Z

Zermatt Close **2** G5
Zetland Road..................**21** D6

HOSPITALS

Acorn Childrens Hospice
...............................**11** A3
Droitwich Spa Hospital ..**16** E4
Evesham Community Hospital
...............................**19** D4
Malvern Community Hospital
...............................**23** D1
Newtown Hospital **8** E5
Pershore Hospital **28** G4
Spire South Bank Hospital
...............................**11** A1
St. Richards Hospice........**8** E6
Tenbury Hospital **29** C3
Waterside Day Hospital..**19** D4
Worcestershire Royal Hospital
...............................**8** E5

POLICE STATIONS

Broadway Police Stn. **29** B2
Droitwich Police Station..**16** E4
Evesham Police Stn. **19** D3
Hindlip Hall (West Mercia
Police Headquarters)**4** F3
Malvern Police Station ..**21** D6
Pershore Police Stn. **28** G4
Tenbury Wells Police Station
...............................**29** B4
Upton upon Severn Police Stn.
...............................**27** C3
Worcester Police Stn. **30** F1

TOURIST INFORMATION CENTRES

Broadway TIC
Tel. 01386 852937 ..**29** B2
Droitwich TIC
Tel. 01905 774312 ..**15** D4
Evesham TIC
Tel. 01386 446944 ..**19** D3
Malvern TIC
Tel. 01684 892289 ..**23** C1
Pershore TIC
Tel. 01386 556591 ..**28** G5
Tenbury Wells TIC
Tel. 01584 810136 ..**29** B4
Upton upon Severn TIC
Tel. 01684 594200 ..**27** B3
Worcester TIC
Tel. 01905 726311 ..**30** G4

SCHOOLS & COLLEGES

Abbey College, The........**26** E4
Abbey Park First &
Nursery Schools **28** F5
Abbey Park Middle School
...............................**28** F5
Badsey First School **17** A6
Bengeworth First Sch. **20** F2
Bishop Perowne College..**7** A1
Blessed Edward Oldcorne
Catholic College **11** A1
Broadheath Primary School
...................................**1** A6
Broadway First School ..**29** C1
Burford Primary School..**29** C3
Callow End Primary School
...............................**13** D3
Chase (Annexe), The **24** F3
Chase, The **24** F3
Chawson Community
First School..............**16** F3
Cherry Orchard First School
...............................**28** G4

Cherry Orchard Prim. School
...............................**11** A2
Christopher Whitehead
Language College **6** F6
Claines Primary School....**3** A2
Colwall Primary School ..**25** A4
Cranham Prim. School **3** D6
Dines Green Primary School
...................................**5** D5
Dodderhill School **15** C5
Droitwich Spa High School
...............................**16** E2
Dyson Perrins High School
...............................**21** D2
Elgar Technology College
...................................**3** B6
Elms School, The **25** A3
Evesham & Malvern Hills Coll.
(Evesham Campus) **19** D5
Evesham & Malvern Hills Coll.
(Malvern Campus)
...............................**23** D1
Evesham High School....**20** E4
Evesham Nursery School
...............................**20** F4
Fairfield Community Primary
School, The **7** D1
Fort Royal Community
Primary School **7** B5
Gorse Hill Community
Primary School..........**7** C2
Grassendale House
Nursery School **23** D1
Great Malvern Primary School
...............................**24** F1
Green Hill School **18** E6
Grove Primary School **22** E5
Hallow Primary School **1** D3
Hindlip First School **3** D2
Holy Redeemer Catholic
Primary School........**28** G5
Kempsey Primary School
...............................**14** G4
Kings Hawford Junior School
...................................**2** G1
Kings St. Albans Junior School
...............................**30** F6
Kings Worcester Senior School
...............................**30** F6
Lyppard Grange Prim. School,
The **8** F3
Madresfield Primary School
...............................**22** H4
Malvern College **23** D3
Malvern College (Hillstone)
...............................**23** C3
Malvern College (The Downs)
...............................**25** B1
Malvern Hills Primary School
...............................**24** G3

Malvern Parish Primary School **24** E2
Malvern St. James (Girls College) **23** D2/**24** E1
Malvern Wells Primary School **26** E4
New College Worcester **11** D2
Northleigh Prim. School..**21** B4
Northwick Manor Inf. School **2** G6
Northwick Manor Junior School **2** G6
Nunnery Wood High School **7** D6
Nunnery Wood Primary School **7** D6
Offenham First School .. **18** G3
Oldbury Park Primary School **6** F4
Our Lady Queen of Peace Catholic Prim. Sch. **6** F6
Perdiswell Prim. School....**3** A6
Perry Wood Primary & Nursery School..........**7** C4
Pershore High School **28** H2
Pinvin First School..........**28** E2
Pitmaston Prim. School **6** F6
Powick Primary School **9** D6
Prince Henrys High School **20** E1
Red Hill Primary School ..**7** B6
Regency High School **7** D1
Regency High School (St. John's Campus) ..**6** F3
Regents Theological College **23** A1
River School, The **3** B3
Riversides School **6** G2
Royal Grammar School (The Grange) **3** B2
Royal Grammar School (Worcester & The Alice Ottley School) **6** H3
Rushwick Prim. School **9** C1
Simon de Montfort Middle School..........**20** E4
Somers Park Primary School **21** D3
Springfield School **6** H3
St. Andrew's First School **19** C4
St. Barnabas Primary School **7** A1
St. Clements Primary School **6** F5
St. Egwin's Middle School **19** D1
St. George's Catholic Primary School..........**6** G2

St. George's Primary School **6** H2
St. James' Prim. School **23** A1
St. Joseph's Catholic Primary School (Droitwich) ..**16** E2
St. Joseph's Catholic Primary School (Worcester) ..**4** E6
St. Joseph's Catholic Primary School (Malvern) **21** C4
St. Mary's Catholic Primary School (Evesham)..**20** E1
St. Mary's Catholic Primary School (Broadway) **29** B2
St. Mary's Convent School **11** B1
St. Matthias Primary School **22** E3
St. Nicholas' Middle School **28** E1
St. Peter's First School ..**16** F5
St. Richard's First School **20** E4
Stanley Road Primary School **7** B5
Swan Lane First Sch. **20** E1
Tenbury High School......**29** B6
Tenbury Prim. School **29** B5
University of Worcester **6** F3
Upton upon Severn Prim. Sch. **27** B3
Vale of Evesham Sch. **20** F4
Warndon Community Primary & Nursery School **8** E1
Westacre Middle Sch. **16** E3
Westlands First School ..**15** C2
Whittington Primary School **12** E3
Witton Middle School......**16** F3
Worcester Coll. of Technology (School of Art & Design) **6** G2
Worcester College of Techology **30** F4
Worcester Sixth Form College **8** E6
Wychbold First & Nursery School........**15** B6
Wyche Primary School ..**23** C5

INDUSTRIAL ESTATES

Aspire Centre, The **29** A3
Atlas Works....................**28** G1
Berkeley Business Park....**4** F6
Berry Hill Ind. Estate **15** B3
Blackmore Park Ind. Estate **24** G6
Blackpole Retail Park **3** C6
Blackpole Trading Estate East **3** C4

Blackpole Trading Estate West **3** C4
Boraston Lane Ind. Estate **29** B3
Bransford Road Ind. Estate **6** E6
Briar Close Business Park **19** D1
British Rail Ind. Estate **7** B4
Bromwich Ind. Estate **10** G2
Buckholt Bus. Centre **3** D5
Canalside Office Complex **30** H2
Carnaud Works **7** C5
Checketts Lane Industrial Area **2** H5
Cosgrove Industrial Area..**3** C5
Countrywide Trading Estate **7** B4
Cranham Estate **3** D5
Defence Evaluation & Research Agency **21** B3/**24** E3
Diglis Industrial Estate....**10** H1
Elgar Business Centre......**1** B2
Elgar Retail Park **3** C6
Enigma Business Park ..**22** G4
Enterprise Centre, The ..**20** F6
Everoak Ind. Estate..........**6** E5
Four Pools Ind. Estate....**20** E5
Great Western Business Park **7** B3
Green Gables Business Centre **20** F1
Gregorys Bank Ind. Area..**6** H1
Grosvenor Business Centre **20** F6
Hampton Lovett Ind. Estate **15** A1
Haysfield Ind. Park **22** F4
Hylton Road Trading Estate **6** F4
Jubilee Works **20** F2
Keytech 7 Business Park **28** H1
Kings Court Business Centre **8** F5
Link Industrial Estate......**21** D4
Link Retail Park, The **20** F5
Lowesmoor Trading Estate **30** H2
Malvern Business Centre **22** G4
Malvern Hills Science Park **24** F3
Malvern Retail Park........**22** G3
Meco Works **6** E5
Merebrook Ind. Estate....**26** H2
Newtown Road Ind. Estate **7** B4

North Street Industrial Estate **15** D4
Orchard Street Ind. Estate **11** A2
Parkridge Retail Park **15** C3
Perdiswell Business Park **3** A4
Perry Wood Trading Estate **7** B5
Pershore Trading Est. **28** H2
Pinvin Industrial Estate ..**28** G2
Pope Iron Road Industrial Area **6** G2
Roman Way Business Park **15** C3
Roman Way Retail Park **15** C3
Sherriff Street Commercial Complex **7** B4
Shire Business Park **4** E5
Shrub Hill Ind. Estate........**7** A4
Six Ways Ind. Estate **24** F2
Spring Lane Ind. Estate..**22** F4
Station Yard Industrial Estate **25** B2
Stonebridge Cross Bus. Park **15** B1
Tenbury Wells Business Park **29** C6
Three Counties Retail Park **22** G3
Three Springs Trading Estate **7** A5
Upper Teme Business Park **29** A3
Upton upon Severn Ind. Estate **27** C3
Vale Business Park **20** F6
Vale Park Business Centre **20** E6
Warndon Business Park ..**4** E5
Waterworks Road Ind. Area **6** G1
Weir Lane Ind. Estate **10** G2
Worcester Porcelain Works **30** G6
Worcester Trade Park **7** B4
Worcester Trading Est. **3** C6